Planet Earth

Planet Earth

Time-Life Books   Alexandria, Virginia

Table of Contents

Planet Earth

"The earth as seen from this distance—nearly a quarter of a million miles—is an unforgettable sight. To begin with, it looks tiny, the size of your thumbnail held at arm's length. It is mostly ocean and clouds, the blue and white dominating the brownish-green of jungles, mountains, and plains.

And does the earth glisten in the sunlight! We think a full moon is very bright, but it's a dullard by comparison. In scientific terms the reflective power of the moon is .07; in other words, its surface absorbs 93 percent of the sunlight and only 7 percent shines back in our eyes. So the earth is a headlight by comparison with the moon. Even the crescent view we are getting now fills our windows with a soft, welcoming light, a beacon beckoning us home."

—Michael Collins

Apollo 11 astronaut, describing the view of Earth from lunar orbit

The space shuttle soars some 200 miles above Earth—often called the blue planet because most of its surface is covered by blue ocean waters. The murky brown patch at the bottom is where the mighty Amazon River dumps its silt into the Atlantic Ocean.

Welcome to Planet Earth

From far away, planet Earth looks like a tiny blue ball floating lazily in space. Up close, however, it is a huge rock with a fiery core, and it is whizzing around the Sun at 106,560 kilometers per hour (66,600 mph)—about fourteen times faster than a speeding bullet.

More than five billion people owe their lives to the planet's perfect features. Orbiting the Sun at an average distance of 149 million km (93 million mi.), Earth is the only planet with just the right temperature for **liquid** water to exist in abundance. Earth's gravity, too, is ideal: It holds in place the **atmosphere** we breathe.

Although Earth began forming about 4.6 billion years ago, most of its surface is much younger. That's because it is constantly being reshaped by volcanoes, earthquakes, storms, **glaciers,** and even drifting continents. These mighty forces—the subjects of this book—play key roles in shaping the world we call home.

Fast FACTS

- Write the number 6,588. Now write 18 zeros after it. That's how many tons Earth weighs!

- Earth is 40,075 km (24,902 mi.) around at its widest point, the equator. Traveling about six kilometers per hour (4 mph), 24 hours a day, you would need nearly nine months to walk around the world.

- There is a tremor—a shift in Earth's crust—once every 30 seconds somewhere on the globe.

- Like an orange being squashed by a hand, Earth is slightly flattened at the poles and bulges slightly at the equator.

- At the planet's core—6,380 km (3,960 mi.) down—the temperature reaches an estimated 6,650°C (12,000°F).

- All the water on Earth was produced during the planet's formation. It has been continuously recycled since then.

Our Place in Space

Spain *(right)* and Morocco *(below)* come to a point—the 37-kilometer-wide (23-mile-wide) Strait of Gibraltar—in this revealing view of the third rock from the Sun. The photo was taken by astronauts orbiting Earth 433 km (269 mi.) above the Atlantic Ocean.

The Solar System

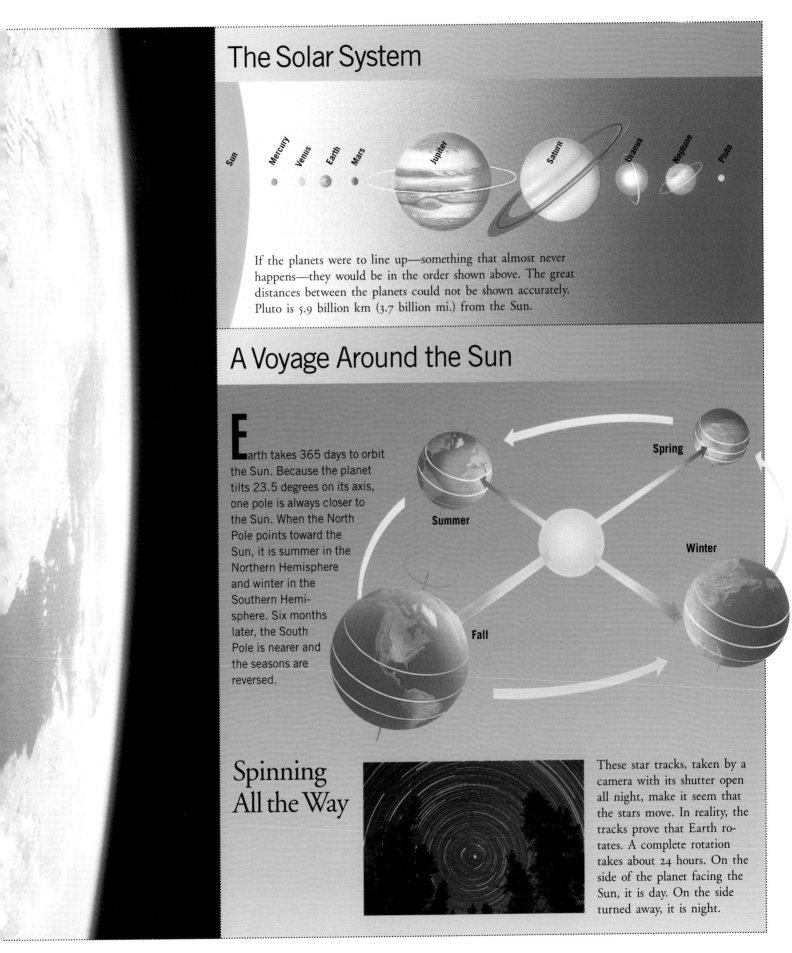

Sun Mercury Venus Earth Mars Jupiter Saturn Uranus Neptune Pluto

If the planets were to line up—something that almost never happens—they would be in the order shown above. The great distances between the planets could not be shown accurately. Pluto is 5.9 billion km (3.7 billion mi.) from the Sun.

A Voyage Around the Sun

Earth takes 365 days to orbit the Sun. Because the planet tilts 23.5 degrees on its axis, one pole is always closer to the Sun. When the North Pole points toward the Sun, it is summer in the Northern Hemisphere and winter in the Southern Hemisphere. Six months later, the South Pole is nearer and the seasons are reversed.

Spring

Summer

Winter

Fall

Spinning All the Way

These star tracks, taken by a camera with its shutter open all night, make it seem that the stars move. In reality, the tracks prove that Earth rotates. A complete rotation takes about 24 hours. On the side of the planet facing the Sun, it is day. On the side turned away, it is night.

How Did Earth Form?

You wouldn't have recognized our solar system when it began forming in a remote corner of the Milky Way galaxy about 4.6 billion years ago. It was just a swirling cloud of gas and dust. But the dust in the cloud was sticky, like snowflakes, and it began to clump together. These clumps then stuck to one another, forming rocky bodies called planetesimals; each was only a few miles wide.

Attracted by gravity, the planetesimals started crashing into each other and sticking together. Over time, they grew into planets. (The planetesimals that did not form planets became asteroids or comets instead.) The newborn planets looked nothing like they do today. Earth, for example, was a giant battered rock. It would take another two and a half billion years to turn into the lush green world we now live on.

With volcanism, plate tectonics, and **erosion** still shaping the modern world, who knows what planet Earth will look like a billion years from now?

The Birth of Earth

4

By the time Earth had reached middle age (about two billion years old), a thick coating of water covered most of its rocky surface. The forces generated by rising currents of heat inside Earth caused the surface to break into a mosaic of huge, slowly creeping land masses called **tectonic plates.** These plates are still on the move, and still molding the face of the planet today.

3

The volcanoes spewed gases that wrapped Earth in a primitive **atmosphere**. One of these gases was water **vapor.** When it hit the frigid temperatures of space, the vapor **condensed** into clouds. From these fell the rains that slowly filled the surface craters with deep oceans. Melting comets also added their water to the oceans.

2

Flying rocks and icy comets bombarded Earth for hundreds of millions of years after the planet first took shape. This cosmic beating pockmarked Earth with craters. The young Earth therefore looked a lot like the Moon does today—except that volcanoes were spouting off all over the globe.

1

Earth's innards 4.5 billion years ago were a bubbling-hot inferno of **liquid** rock. Heavy **elements** such as iron and nickel sank to the center, forming a solid core. Lighter materials—mainly white-hot silicon and aluminum—floated to the surface. Where the crust was thin, liquid rock gushed out as **lava** from volcanoes. A thin ring circled Earth, made up of debris left over from when the planets were first forming.

A Look Inside

Like the skin of an apple, Earth's crust is a very thin cover. Below the crust is the thicker **mantle,** a layer of rock so hot that it behaves like melted plastic. Closer to the center is a fluid outer core, which is made of melted iron and other elements, including sulfur. It surrounds the inner core—a solid iron **crystal** the size of the Moon that completes its daily rotation almost one second faster than the rest of the planet.

Crust
Mantle
Outer Core
Inner Core

Look Out Below!

Slam a 300,000-ton ball of nickel and iron into the planet and you'll wind up with a pit like this one—Meteor Crater in Arizona, formed by a meteorite impact 50,000 years ago. The crater is over 1,200 m (4,000 ft.) wide and 168 m (550 ft.) deep. Twenty football games could be played on the floor of the crater—all at the same time!

Continents Adrift

Australia and Antarctica have become one continent. A new ocean has formed in East Africa. And California is part of a mountain chain in Alaska.

Those statements will be true—150 million years from now, that is—if experts on the theory called **continental drift** are correct. These scientists believe that Earth's seven continents were once fused into a single landmass, called Pangaea. The world's seawater was held in one huge ocean, Panthalassa. About 152 million years ago, Pangaea started to slowly break apart. Like rafts of rock riding on a layer of semimelted stone, the continents began creeping toward their present positions.

Study a globe and you will see that the continents would fit together like pieces of a jigsaw puzzle. The east coasts of South and North America could interlock with the west coast of Africa, while Greenland could fit into eastern Canada.

Fossils—the preserved remains of age-old plants and animals—are another clue that continental drift took place. Identical fossils of Glossopteris (a tropical plant) and Lystrosaurus (a reptile) have been found in both Africa and Antarctica. This suggests that the two continents were once joined. Imagine that—a hot day on the icy continent of Antarctica!

Strange But TRUE!

Please Pass the Possum!

The opossum *(below)* is North America's only marsupial (a mammal that carries its young in a stomach pouch). All other marsupials—including kangaroos, wombats, and koalas—live only in and near Australia. This coincidence supports the scientific view that marsupials migrated to Australia before it became the island it is today.

People   Alfred Wegener

The notion that continents might rip in half was a wild one when Alfred Wegener *(above)* proposed it in 1912. Aware that fossils recently discovered in Africa matched those in Brazil, Wegener argued that all the world's landmasses had belonged to a "supercontinent," Pangaea. But some force, said Wegener, had caused the continents to go their separate ways.

Wegener spent the next 18 years looking for clues to support his theory. Trying to set up an observatory in Greenland in 1930, Wegener got caught in a snowstorm and died from exposure. Not until the 1960s, when geologists began to realize that Earth's crust is made of moving plates, did Wegener's ideas catch on.

425 Million Years Ago

According to the theory of continental drift, most land-masses were clustered in the southern part of the globe 425 million years ago. North America and Europe lay side by side along the equator.

255 Million Years Ago

By about 255 million years ago, the continents had moved together to form a single landmass called Pangaea. Animals migrated freely from one part of this supercontinent to another.

94 Million Years Ago

North America and Eurasia had moved apart, forming the North Atlantic. The gap between Africa and South America had become the South Atlantic. Australia and Antarctica still touched; India had split from Africa.

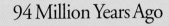

Continents on the Move!

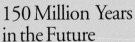

150 Million Years in the Future

Geologists predict that Africa will drift north, squeezing the Mediterranean Sea to a channel. East Africa will split off from the main continent, creating a new ocean.

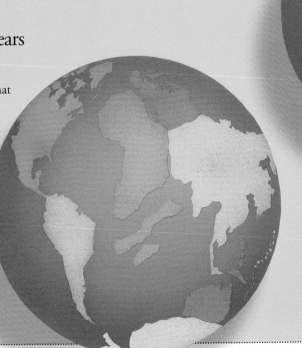

Present

North and South America continue to move away from Europe at the rate of 4 cm (1.5 in.) per year. At the same time, India is moving into Asia at 5 cm (2 in.) per year.

What Is Plate Tectonics?

Plate tectonics is the study of the moving plates that make up Earth's crust. ("Tekton" is the Greek word for "to build.") Slowly creeping over the surface of the globe at 1 to 10 cm (⅓ to 4 in.) per year, these 50- to 80-kilometer-thick (30- to 50-mile-thick) plates carry continents, seafloor, or both. The North American plate stretches 10,000 km (6,200 mi.) from California to Iceland, while the Juan de Fuca plate, off Washington State, is just 500 km (310 mi.) wide.

Like graham crackers riding on bubbling-hot oatmeal, the plates float on a superheated "sea" of partly melted rock that lies just beneath the planet's crust. The plates crash head-on, pull apart, or rub each other the wrong way, causing all sorts of geologic phenomena—including earthquakes and mountain-building—to occur along their edges. One plate may even push another back down into Earth, giving rise to volcanoes.

The San Andreas fault *(left)* is a strike-slip fault that runs about 1,200 km (750 mi.) from the Gulf of California to Cape Mendocino. Like a never-healing scar on Earth's surface, it shows where the Pacific plate is grinding its way northwest past the North American plate. The movement builds up incredible strain wherever the jagged edges of the two plates lock together. When one plate lurches past the other to a new position, shock waves—also called earthquakes—fan out from the point of rupture.

SEAFLOOR SPREADING

When two oceanic plates move away from each other, Earth's crust may crack and ooze **magma**, creating volcanic islands, called seamounts, or new seafloor.

SUBDUCTION

When oceanic plates collide, one dives below the other and volcanoes result. If the **lava** breaks the surface and piles up, a volcanic island forms. The islands of Japan formed this way.

Disunited Plates

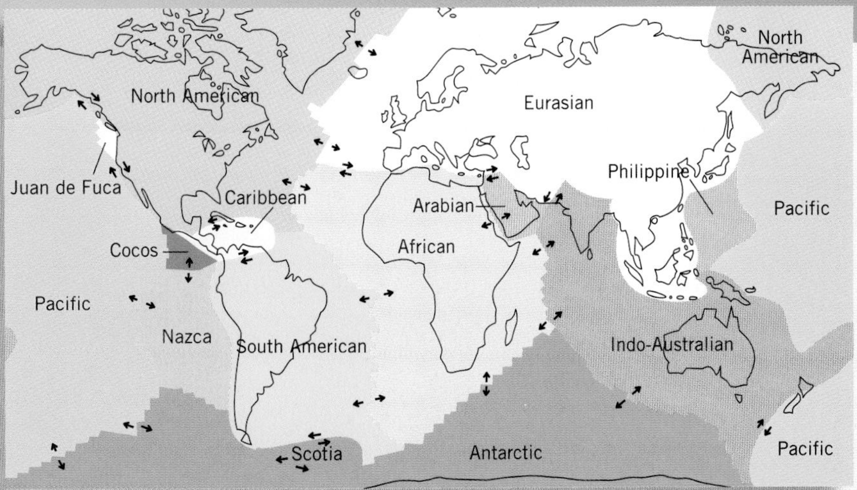

All sorts of geologic mayhem breaks out along the edges of Earth's 14 major **tectonic plates,** shown at right. More than half of all volcanoes erupt along the borders of the Pacific plate. The highest mountain range on Earth—the Himalayas—was thrust up when the Indo-Australian plate plowed into the Eurasian plate. The deepest spot in the ocean—the Mariana Trench, 11,035 m (36,205 ft.)—is where the Philippine and the Pacific plates collide.

North American

Juan de Fuca

Cocos

Pacific

Nazca

South American

Caribbean

Scotia

Eurasian

African

Arabian

Antarctic

Philippine

Pacific

Indo-Australian

North American

Pacific

SUBDUCTION

On hitting a lighter continental plate, a heavy oceanic plate slides down, or is **subducted,** into the **mantle.** There the plate edge melts, and the magma rises to the surface through volcanoes.

STRIKE-SLIP FAULT

Crustal plates do more than collide and pull apart. Along a strike-slip fault they move sidelong, grinding their edges as they pass. The friction that builds up causes tremors and earthquakes.

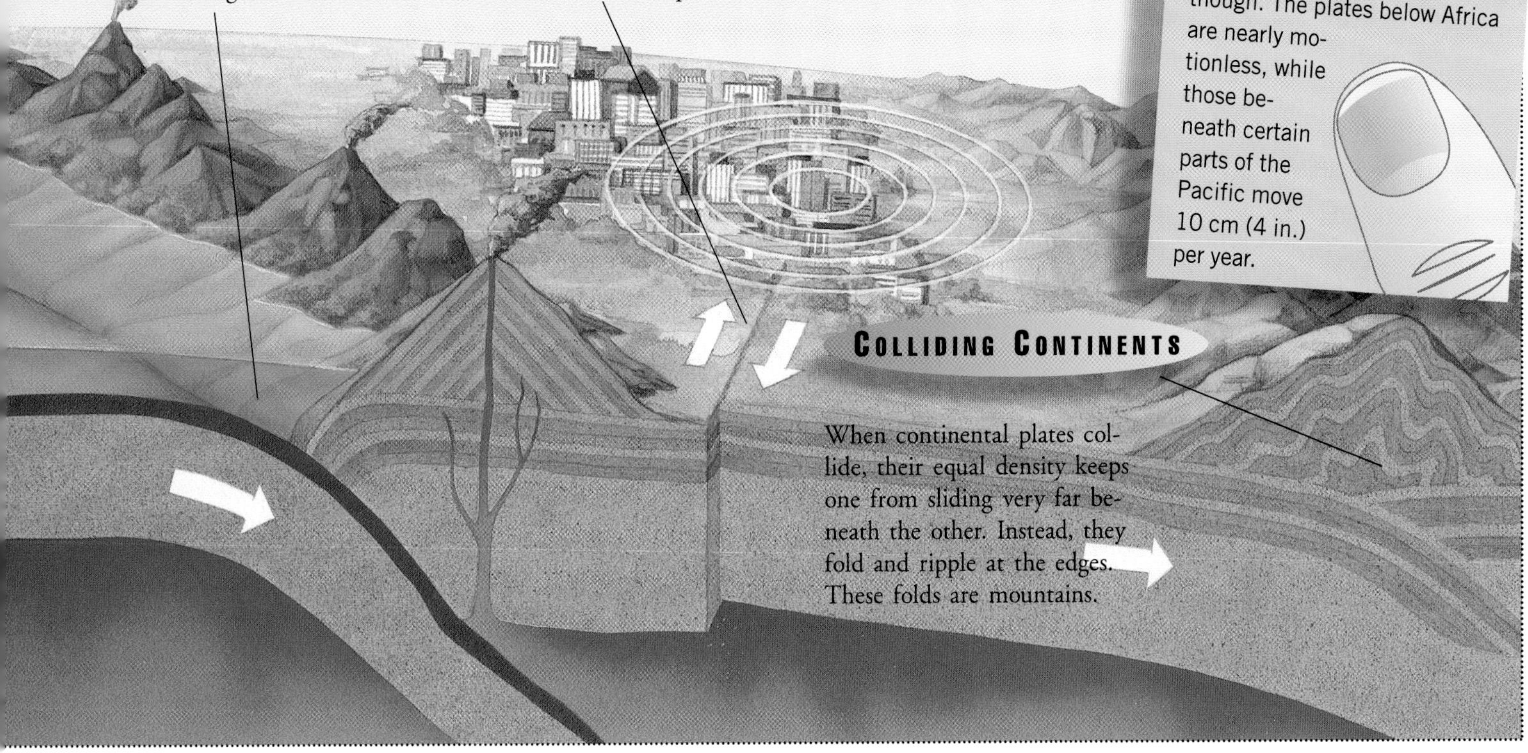

How Fast?

What does Earth's crust have in common with your fingernail? Speed! The plates that carry the world's continents and oceans move at the same average rate—about 3 cm (1 in.) per year—that your nails grow. There are a few exceptions, though. The plates below Africa are nearly motionless, while those beneath certain parts of the Pacific move 10 cm (4 in.) per year.

COLLIDING CONTINENTS

When continental plates collide, their equal density keeps one from sliding very far beneath the other. Instead, they fold and ripple at the edges. These folds are mountains.

What Makes Mountains?

Like earthquakes and volcanoes, mountains are formed by the violent interplay of Earth's moving plates. These plates are made of solid rock, but they buckle and twist like slabs of warm clay when they collide. The name for this mountain-building process is **orogeny** (from the Greek words for "mountain" and "growth").

Mountains take shape in one of three basic ways. Folded mountains result from the collision of two continental plates. Like the folds that appear in cloth napkins when you slide them against each other on a flat surface, the crust of both colliding plates simply wrinkles up.

Volcanic mountains are formed when a plate carrying seafloor hits a plate carrying land. The oceanic plate, being denser, is driven beneath the continental plate. The leading edge of the oceanic plate dives deep into the **mantle,** where it melts. The **magma** then works its way to the surface, creating a chain of volcanic mountains.

Fault-block mountains occur when the crust is broken by a fault and one block moves up relative to the other.

Folded Mountains

Folded mountains take shape wherever two continental plates ram into each other, compressing and uplifting the rock they carry *(diagram below)*. Depending on the type of rock and the intensity of the collision, the folds may range in height from a few feet to several miles. The Appalachians in the United States, the Alps in Europe, and the Himalayas in Asia are all folded mountain ranges

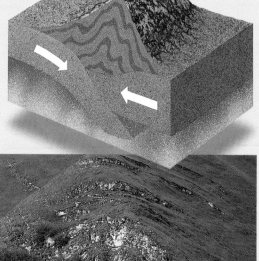

A folded mountain, like the peak in the Pyrenees shown below, looks like twisted taffy.

Would You Believe?

Many mountaintops were once ocean bottoms. Want proof? Consider ammonites, the coiled mollusks that lived in the ocean during the Mesozoic Era but died out about 65 million years ago. Ammonite fossils like the one at left have been found in both the Himalaya and Rocky Mountains—proof that the seafloors of yesteryear are now sky-high.

Volcanic Mountains

Volcanic mountains often mark the spot where an oceanic plate has met its match—a high-riding continental plate. The denser, heavier oceanic plate is pushed down into the fiery-hot mantle. Its edge melts into magma, or molten rock, which forces its way to the surface as a volcano *(diagram below)*. The Cascades (in Washington, Oregon, and California) and the high peaks of the Andes (in South America) are both volcanic ranges.

Sunrise lights the jagged peaks of the Tetons *(above)*, a fault-block range in Wyoming.

Popocatepetl *(below)* is an active volcano in Mexico. Its name means "smoking mountain" in Aztec. It is 5,451 m (17,887 ft.) high.

Fault-Block Mountains

Fault-block mountains form at the seam along which two continental plates are separating *(diagram above)*. As the rocks move away from each other, they thin and crack. Huge chunks of stone then collapse into the hollow between them. The rock that remains at the upper level is called a horst; the rock that subsides to a lower level is a graben.

Mountains Close Up

The fact that Mount Everest is Earth's highest peak was not discovered until 1852. In that year, a survey clerk in India, working on sightings made four years earlier, found to his surprise that "Peak XV" on the Nepal/Tibet border was nearly 300 m (1,000 ft.) taller than its neighbors. (It lay hidden behind nearer, seemingly higher mountains.) Named for British surveyor George Everest, Mount Everest became the goal of mountaineers worldwide. Starting in 1921, they launched a total of 11 assaults on the peak before Edmund Hillary and Tenzing Norgay *(opposite page)* reached the summit on May 29, 1953.

What It Takes

Wearing a metallic mask to protect his face from frostbite and solar radiation, American climber Rick Ridgeway slogs toward the crest of 8,610-meter-high (28,250-foot-high) K-2, the world's second-highest peak, on September 6, 1978. His gear included bottled water to battle dehydration, safety ropes, an ice ax for cutting steps in slippery slopes, and boots with crampons (cleats for ice and snow). Finding a place to pitch your tent is not easy up this high!

Although mountains tower above every continent, Asia has 14 peaks over 8,000 m (26,250 ft.). This drawing compares Mount Everest with the tallest peaks on four other continents.

How Tall?

Everest, Nepal/Tibet
8,848 m (29,028 ft.)

Aconcagua, Argentina
6,959 m (22,831 ft.)

McKinley, Alaska
6,194 m (20,320 ft.)

Kilimanjaro, Tanzania
5,895 m (19,341 ft.)

Elbrus, Russia
5,642 m (18,510 ft.)

Tall—and Still Growing!

Because India is slamming into Asia at a speed of 5 cm (2 in.) per year, Mount Everest *(below, right)* and its fellow Himalayas are growing higher every day! Everest gains an estimated 1 cm (⅜ in.) per year.

Two Who Got to the Top

Here's what you must overcome to reach the top of the world: steep and icy **glaciers**, deep crevasses, avalanches, gale-force **winds**, blinding snowstorms, lack of oxygen, dehydration, disorientation, and hypothermia. No surprise, then, that it took two very special people—Edmund Hillary, a New Zealand beekeeper, and Tenzing Norgay, a Sherpa guide from Nepal—to reach the summit of Everest first. Their success, on May 29, 1953, came after 32 years of failed tries that included the deaths of 16 men. Here's how Hillary described the final moments of the climb: "I suddenly realize that the ridge above me doesn't go up, but goes down. There, there just above me, is a softly rounded, snow-covered little bump, as big as a haystack. The summit. We stagger up the final stretch. We are there. Nothing above us, a world below. I felt no elation at first, just relief and a sense of wonder."

What Causes Erosion?

Shaping Monument Valley

Erosion is the scraping and polishing of Earth's surface by water, wind, and ice. It works in tandem with force called **weathering,** which does the heavy work of breaking large rocks into little pieces. Together, **erosion** and weathering create some of Earth's most pleasing features, such as caves, canyons, and pillars of rock hundreds of meters high.

Water, dripping as a liquid or bulldozing its way as a frozen glacier, can grind down even the tallest mountain. Wind is a scouring agent, too: It carries tiny rocks at high speed, acting like a sandblaster to carve the stone in its path into odd and eerie shapes.

Erosion and weathering do more than sculpt the planet. They also produce the rich **loess** soil that gives rise to bountiful crops. Seen that way, the two forces help sustain life on Earth.

1

Arizona's Monument Valley started out as a level plain on the Colorado Plateau. About 65 million years ago, the entire plateau began to rise. As it did, rivers eroded channels in the rock.

65 Million Years Ago

2

Millions of years went by, and the rivers continued to cut valleys in the rock. Water worked its erosional magic in other ways, too. Carbonic acid—a natural ingredient of rain—ate away at the rock. Water also pooled in crevices, then shattered the rock as it froze and expanded.

20 to 30 Million Years Ago

3

Strong winds blew sand and dust across the plateau. This wore away exposed layers of softer rock, but the winds could not touch the columns of hard red sandstone. Today these columns are the mesas and buttes that rise above the floor of Monument Valley.

Today

Would You Believe?

Cone Home

For 2,000 years, people in the Turkish province of Cappadocia lived, worked, and went to school in carved-out rock formations called "fairy chimneys" *(right)*. The towers are made of a soft volcanic rock, known as tuff, that was eroded over millenniums. The inside was perfect for scooping out—and moving into! Whole cities of these excavated cones were inhabited as recently as 1923.

Mechanical Weathering

If your bike has ever hit a pothole *(below),* you know all about mechanical weathering. This type of weathering occurs when a mechanical process, such as the repeated freezing and thawing of water, loosens a material such as stone or asphalt, then breaks it into smaller and smaller pieces. Other examples of mechanical weathering include heating and cooling—and even an invasion by plant roots!

Ice

Chemical Weathering

Both the Devil's Marbles in Australia *(below)* and the decrepit truck shown above got that way through oxidation— that is, they rusted! Oxidation is an example of chemical weathering, in which an object undergoes a chemical change that makes it erode. In the case of the Devil's Marbles, silicate minerals are decomposing in the rock, causing large pieces to flake off. The same process turns an iron truck to dust—but it takes many decades!

The Left and Right Mittens *(below, center)* are buttes in Monument Valley, Arizona. Some area Indians call the formations "rain barrels" and leave offerings nearby to bring rain to the desert.

What Makes Rivers?

Most rivers begin as rain or snow that falls at high elevations. (**Precipitation** is heavier on the windward side of a mountain range, so the majority of rivers begin there.) Other rivers get their start when water melts from a glacier or comes bubbling up out of the ground.

Whatever the source, the water takes the shortest and easiest path downhill. It starts out as tiny rivulets, which run together to form small streams, which in turn merge to make a mighty river. Rushing downhill, the current rips sand, clay, and gravel from the river's banks. These particles become erosive teeth that gnaw valleys, canyons, and waterfalls in the land.

The Mississippi is a good example of a large river. From its source, a lake in northern Minnesota, the Mississippi River drains an area of 3.25 million sq. km (1.25 million sq. mi.)—about 40 percent of the United States. It carries away 600 million tons of sediment each year. Far downstream at its mouth, the river fans out and breaks into channels, then dumps its silty load into the Gulf of Mexico.

A Continental Divide

The crest of the Rockies is often called a "continental divide" because rain falling east of it drains into the Atlantic or the Arctic, while rainfall to the west drains into the Pacific. The drainage areas for the three oceans are shown at right.

Arctic Ocean

Pacific Ocean

Atlantic Ocean

Water flows in opposite directions from a continental divide.

From Source to Sea

A river's source, or starting point, is usually a glacier or small spring high in the mountains. The water rushes downhill from there, joining with other streams and gouging out rapids, waterfalls, and gorges until it reaches the transition zone—a fairly level area where the current loses speed. During floods, water covers the flood plain, depositing sediment and forming swamps. Any remaining sediment is dumped at the mouth, or delta, where the river reaches the ocean.

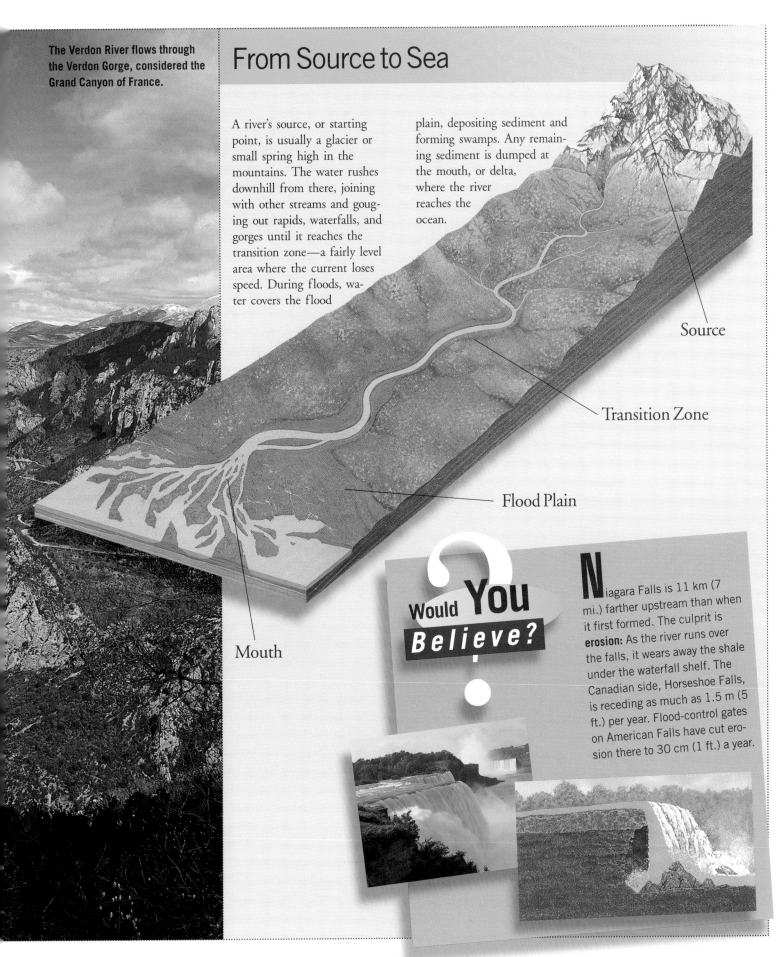

Source

Transition Zone

Flood Plain

Mouth

Would You Believe?

Niagara Falls is 11 km (7 mi.) farther upstream than when it first formed. The culprit is **erosion:** As the river runs over the falls, it wears away the shale under the waterfall shelf. The Canadian side, Horseshoe Falls, is receding as much as 1.5 m (5 ft.) per year. Flood-control gates on American Falls have cut erosion there to 30 cm (1 ft.) a year.

What Shapes Canyons?

Grand Canyon National Park, Arizona, USA

The Grand Canyon is well named: At 445 km (277 mi.) long, 1.6 km (1 mi.) deep, and 30 km (18 mi.) wide, it is the grandest canyon on Earth. The chasm began to form about 10 million years ago, when the Pacific plate crashed into—and dived under—the North American plate. As the Rocky Mountains rose, the Colorado River rushed downhill; the river soon cut a groove that would grow into a canyon.

Modern visitors to the canyon can see almost half of Earth's geologic history on display. The river's steady flow has exposed layers of rock that range from 1.7 billion years old at the bottom to 225 million years old at the top (because of **erosion,** the rocks you see at the top are this old.) They tell the saga of a region that has gone from being a warm, shallow ocean to a barren, dry desert.

Now a national park, the Grand Canyon is also home to a tribe of Native Americans, the Havasupai. Their land includes a waterfall believed to have healing powers.

Time Travel—Through Solid Rock!

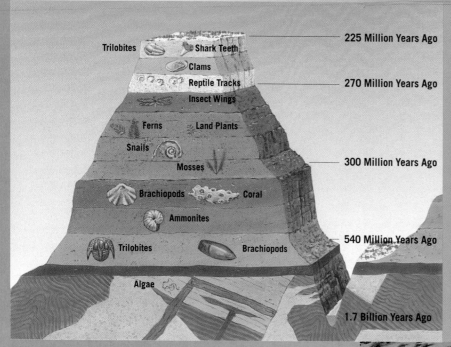

Trilobites — Shark Teeth — 225 Million Years Ago
Clams
Reptile Tracks — 270 Million Years Ago
Insect Wings
Ferns — Land Plants
Snails
Mosses — 300 Million Years Ago
Brachiopods — Coral
Ammonites
Trilobites — Brachiopods — 540 Million Years Ago
Algae
1.7 Billion Years Ago

Studying Earth's History Layer by Layer

It took the Colorado River 10 million years to gouge the Grand Canyon to its present depth of 1.6 km (1 mi.). In doing so, the river exposed nearly 2 billion years of geologic history *(left)*. Many of the exposed rock layers contain fossils—the preserved remains of plants and animals that lived when sediment (now rock) was being laid down.

U.S. Geological Survey
Flagstaff, Arizona

In the grand scheme of things, the Grand Canyon is no big deal—there's one on Mars that is as long as the United States is wide! Called Valles Marineris, the Martian gorge was discovered by—and named after—NASA's Mariner spacecraft. Valles Marineris is 6.5 km (4 mi.) deep, 240 km (150 mi.) wide, and 4,800 km (3,000 mi.) long. It probably formed when volcanoes rose, stretching and cracking the surface.

What Is a Desert?

Deserts don't have to be hot! Antarctica is one, yet temperatures there reach -58.2°C (-72°F). Nor do they have to be sandy: There's not a dune in sight on 85 percent of the world's deserts.

The one thing these regions do have in common is dryness: A desert is a large land area that gets less than 25 cm (10 in.) of rain per year. Deserts cover one-fifth of Earth's land and are on all continents but Europe.

The ideal place for a desert to form is an area that lies too far from the ocean to get rain or an area in the "rain shadow" of a mountain range. The driest desert—Chile's Atacama—has droughts lasting hundreds of years. The largest desert, the Sahara, would cover the continental United States.

Desert plants have adapted to little water in fascinating ways. Some dig deep for moisture; mesquite-tree roots may reach down 52 m (175 ft.). Others, such as the cactus, have pleated skins that expand to store water.

Dunes of Doom

Like the arms of an invading ocean, sand dunes slowly submerged this oasis in Egypt's Western Desert. Its people were forced to leave.

Deserts gobble a total of 120,000 square km (46,000 square mi.) of land—an area the size of Pennsylvania—each year. The spread is partly natural, but it is also caused by overgrazing and overpopulation. When herd animals eat the vegetation that anchors sandy soil, the soil becomes loose and blows away. As the wind continues to blow, sand dunes take shape and migrate—that is, they move back and forth across the land. This makes life a struggle for people trying to survive at the desert's edge.

Haboob Ahead!

Kicking up a stinging wall of sand hundreds of feet high, a **haboob,** or desert windstorm, roars across the Sahara. A haboob occurs when a monsoon (a seasonal rainstorm) meets dry air currents swirling above it. It's easy to see how this violent storm gave us the English word *hubbub,* meaning "loud confusion."

Strange But TRUE!

Shipwreck in the Sand

In 1912, the German cargo ship *Eduard Bohlen* ran aground on the Atlantic coast of Africa. Today it lies buried by sand, not sea: The shipwreck *(right)* sits in the sand of southern Africa's Namib Desert, more than 1.5 km (1 mi.) inland. This proves that the Namib is migrating west into the ocean, extending the continent's coastline as it goes.

Meet the Dune Family!

Most sand dunes belong to one of three main categories, described below. Each type of dune is caused by a unique combination of environmental factors, such as topography, wind, and vegetation.

Barchans

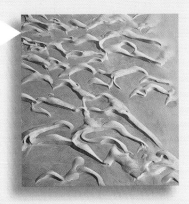

Barchans are sand dunes shaped like crescents. Formed when sand blows across a flat desert floor, they move and change shape rapidly. The horns, or crescent tips, point downwind.

Seifs

Seifs (from the Arab word for "sword") are long, slender dunes with sharp crests. The point of each seif faces into the wind. Each shift in the wind's direction causes a new squiggle to form at the end of the dune.

Star Dunes

A star dune is a group of barchan dunes that have merged to form a star shape. Star dunes form in places where the wind is always changing direction; as a result, they do not migrate.

Land Carved by Glaciers

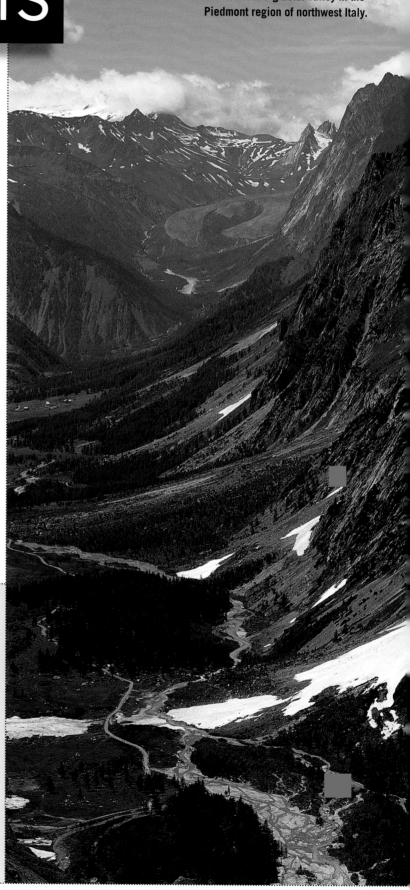

Val Ferret is a glacial valley in the Piedmont region of northwest Italy.

Glaciers are lumbering blocks of ice that slowly carve the face of our planet. Found on every continent but Australia, they cover about 10 percent of Earth's land surface.

The biggest **glaciers,** called continental ice sheets, are massive slabs of ice that blanket an entire continent, such as Antarctica. The Antarctic ice sheet covers 12.5 million square km (5 million sq. mi.) of land; in some places, it reaches a depth of 3,000 m (9,850 ft.). Mountain glaciers, though smaller, are more numerous; about 100,000 of them exist worldwide. A mountain glacier forms at a high elevation, then grinds downhill under its own weight. As it crawls across the earth, the glacier creates its own souvenir of the trip: a U-shaped valley.

Continental ice sheets and mountain glaciers are both made from snow. When powdery snow is crushed by the weight of new snow falling on top of it, it slowly changes to **firn**—dense, tightly packed snow. Repeated melting and freezing, combined with growing pressure from the overlying snow, turns the firn into clear, hard glacial ice (much like the ice cubes from a freezer).

The birth of a glacier may take just 20 years—or several thousand!

What's a Fjord?

A fjord is a valley that has been scooped out by a glacier, then flooded by the sea. This one-two punch forms a long, deep, narrow ocean inlet. Geiranger Fjord, shown at left, is in Norway; fjords are also found in Chile, New Zealand, Canada, and the United States.

How Ice Carves Earth

A glacier usually takes shape in a **cirque**—a bowl-shaped area near the top of a mountain. Tugged by the force of gravity, the glacier begins to "flow" downhill a meter or so per day, gouging out a valley as it goes. It picks up anything in its path—dirt, rocks, boulders—and carries it along.

Some glaciers flow all the way to the sea, but others "retreat"—that is, melt—back up the valley they carved. If the ice in a cirque melts, it forms a mountain lake that feeds a fast-flowing river.

Strange But TRUE!

The Iceman Waketh

Perfectly preserved by a glacier, the "Iceman"—the oldest intact skeleton ever found—lies where he fell some 5,200 years ago. The body, believed to be that of a shepherd killed by an avalanche during Europe's Copper Age, was in excellent condition because the glacial ice had turned it into a mummy.

The Galloping Glacier

The Hubbard Glacier *(right)* is one of Alaska's largest—and fastest! Nicknamed "the galloping glacier," it migrates toward the ocean at 55 m (180 ft.) per day. Upon reaching Disenchantment Bay, the Hubbard "calves" icebergs— that is, it drops huge chunks of ice from its snout into the sea.

What Makes Caves?

Stalactites adorn the Grotte de Clamouse, a cave in France.

Caves are carved by water. After mixing with carbon dioxide in the air or soil to form carbonic acid, water can dissolve as much as .25 cm (1/10 in.) of soft limestone per year. The result is an underground cavity hollowed out by chemical **erosion.**

A cave may extend more than 32 km (20 mi.) into the earth. Its passages may be wider than an interstate or so narrow that not even a six-year-old could wriggle through them. The largest known cave—Sarawak Chamber on the island of Borneo—could hold 800 tennis courts!

In addition to scooping out subterranean rooms, dripping water builds some fantastic formations: With a little imagination, you can see organ pipes, pearls, butterflies, melting candles, and even strips of bacon and frying eggs. This decorative power is shown at right. Minerals deposited by dripping water have created stalactites—they look like stone icicles—that slowly descend from the ceiling. Water dripping onto the floor, meanwhile, has deposited steadily rising stalagmites. When a stalactite meets a stalagmite, they fuse into a column—but the process may take 100,000 years.

Just Add Water!

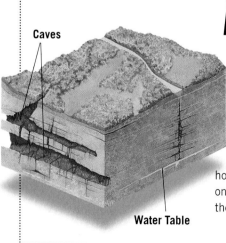

Caves

Water Table

A cave is created by the interaction of water and rock. As rainfall seeps through bedrock, it absorbs carbon dioxide gas from the soil. This turns the water into carbonic acid, which eats away the soft limestone underground. As a result, hollows form in the earth. Later on, the water table drops and the cave dries out.

Strange But TRUE!

Keep Him in the Dark!

The Texas blind salamander (*right*) lives only in caves, so it has never developed a sense of sight. To find its prey, the 10-centimeter-long (4-inch-long) amphibian relies on signals it receives from sensory organs on its head and sides. The creature's colorless skin lacks pigment because it needs no protection from the sun.

A wild horse gallops away from its pursuers in this 17,000-year-old wall painting from the Lascaux Cave in southern France. Four boys discovered the cave—and its treasure-trove of primitive paintings—on September 12, 1940. They were out on a fox hunt that day when their dog, Robot, fell into a hole and disappeared. In the course of rescuing Robot, the boys stumbled across the richest cache of prehistoric art ever found.

Towers Made of Stone

The same forces that create caves formed China's Guilin Mountains *(above)*. First, an ancient river carved a V-shaped valley in the earth. The river then eroded the land for thousands of years, dissolving the bedrock but leaving fertile farmland—and these 200-meter-high (650-foot-high) limestone towers—in its wake.

What Are Lakes?

Lakes occupy less than two percent of Earth's surface, yet they help sustain human life. They give us fish to eat and water to drink. They carry cargo ships and irrigate crops in the field. They remove wastes, generate electrical power, and provide recreation for millions of people.

A large lake is like an ocean: Waves tower 15 m (50 ft.) high at its center during severe storms, and the lake holds so much water that it affects the local **weather.** Indeed, the world's largest saltwater lake, with a surface area of 679,000 square km (262,000 sq. mi.), is called the Caspian Sea.

The largest freshwater lake is the aptly named Lake Superior on the Michigan-Canada border. Measurements of the deepest lake—Baikal, in eastern Siberia—vary according to how they are made; counting its silt-filled abyss adds 320 m (1,051 ft.) to its official depth. Dating back 25 million years, Baikal is the world's oldest lake.

How Deep?

The world's deepest lake, at 1,620 m (5,314 ft.), is Russia's Lake Baikal. It contains as much water as all five Great Lakes combined. Of those, Lake Superior is the deepest, at 393 m (1,290 ft.); Lake Erie, just 64 m (210 ft.) deep, is the shallowest. Together, the six lakes hold 40 percent of all the fresh water in the world.

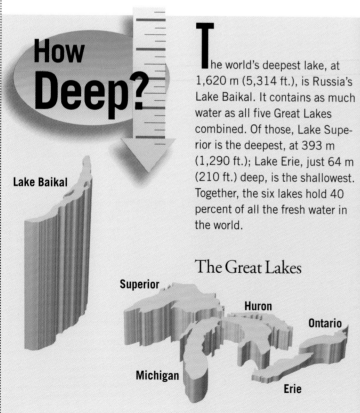

Lake Baikal

The Great Lakes

Superior

Huron

Ontario

Michigan

Erie

Glacial debris suspended in Canada's Peyto Lake turns the water bright blue.

The Look of Lakes

Rift Valley Lake

When two continental plates pull apart, a wedge of land often collapses between them. If water then fills the gap, it forms a rift valley lake.

Crater Lake

A crater lake forms when the caldera (a collapsed cone) of an extinct volcano fills with water. This is how Oregon's Crater Lake came to be.

Oxbow Lake

As a river meanders, it makes noose-shaped loops. The water may then take a shortcut, chopping free the loop to form an oxbow lake.

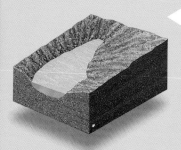

Deflation Lake

A deflation lake, or oasis, begins when desert winds erode a hollow in the sand. If the hollow drops as low as the water table, it fills with liquid.

Tarn

Meltwater that fills a **cirque**—a high basin scooped out by a moving glacier—is called a tarn, or mountain lake.

Would You Believe?

Some people think this photo, snapped by Sandra Mansi at Lake Champlain, Vermont, on July 5, 1977, shows a monster nicknamed Champ. Lake monsters have also been reported in Okanagan Lake, British Columbia, and in Scotland's notorious Loch Ness.

What Is a Volcano?

Have you ever opened a soda bottle that's been shaken up? If so, you have seen how an explosive volcanic eruption works. Like the gas trapped in soda, the gases in the molten rock called **magma** can explosively tear the magma apart as it erupts out of the volcano.

The bottom of a volcano's "soda bottle" lies tens to hundreds of kilometers below Earth's surface, where temperatures are between 600° and 1,200°C (1,100° and 2,200°F) and some rocks melt like butter in a hot pan. The molten rock rises toward the surface and collects in the crust, in pools called magma reservoirs. A central vent connects the magma reservoir with the volcano's summit crater. Some volcanoes will have one or more side vents as well.

Steam, ash, and gas erupting from a volcano can rise in a tall eruption cloud. Sometimes this cloud of particles collapses, becoming a dangerous **pyroclastic flow** ("pyroclastic" means "broken by fire"), a hot cloud of gas, ash, and pumice that rushes down the mountain at breakneck speed, incinerating everything in its path.

What's in a Name?

Volcano

About 20 centuries ago, a hilly island in the Mediterranean Sea near Sicily began to belch smoke and fire. To explain this odd event, people said the mountain held the workshop of Vulcan, blacksmith of the Roman gods. The ash clouds, they said, were smoke from his furnace, and the fiery chunks of **lava,** sparks from his anvil. They named the island "Vulcano," from which came the word "volcano."

Eruption Cloud

Summit Crater

Central Vent

Pyroclastic Flow

Side Vents

Magma Reservoir

Mount Nyamlagira, in Congo, spews out a river of fiery lava.

Red Lava vs. Ash Volcano

Magmas erupt in many ways, depending on what's in them. Those containing little gas flow downhill as glowing lava (*left*). Magmas rich in gas erupt violently, as the trapped gases expand rapidly in Earth's atmosphere, blasting the magma into billions of particles, large and small. These particles fall back to Earth's surface and form a pyroclastic-fall blanket, piling up thickest near the vent. Below, ash from a volcano in Iceland darkens the snow.

Where Do Volcanoes Form?

Most of Earth's 1,400 or so active volcanoes are in places where two **tectonic plates** meet *(pages 14-15)*. When the dense, oceanic part of one plate hits the lighter, dry-land portion of another plate, the denser edge dives under the other plate. This is called **subduction.** Part of the sinking edge melts into **magma,** which rises in hot, gooey bubbles and breaks through the plate above it. This action created the Andes Mountains in South America.

When two plates move away from each other, cracks open in the crust. If the cracks are below the sea, magma rises through the cracks along a spreading ridge, to form new ocean floor or volcanic islands (Iceland is an example). If the boundary between the two plates is on land, the magma builds volcanoes on a rift-valley floor.

"Hot spot" volcanoes, such as those in Hawaii, occur in the middle of a plate, not at the edge. Like a candle flame melting holes in a bar of wax, the hot spot's plume of hot mantle material burns through the plate above it.

Fast FACTS

Where the Active Volcanoes Are

An "active" volcano is one that has erupted in the past 10,000 years. (A volcano that has been quiet for that period is called "extinct.") Most of the world's 1,400 or so active volcanoes are in just a few countries. At right are the eight countries with the most volcanoes.

Russia—171	
Indonesia—161	
U.S.A.—146	
Japan—119	
Chile—110	
Ethiopia—72	
Philippines—53	
Iceland—33	

SHIELD

A shield volcano has shallow slopes and a broad base. This is because shield volcanoes mainly erupt runny **lava**, which generally flows long distances before cooling off and hardening. Many of Earth's hot spots contain shield volcanoes, like the Hawaiian volcano Kilauea seen at left.

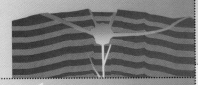

COMPOSITE

Composite volcanoes such as Japan's Mount Fuji *(left)* are common in subduction zones, where one plate dives under another. Such volcanoes have steep slopes made of alternating layers of lava and ash.

CINDER CONE

A cinder cone volcano with a bowl-shaped crater rises above a dark lava flow in Paricutín, Mexico *(left)*. This volcano's steep sides were built by cinders flung into the sky.

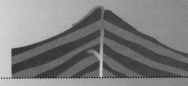

Pacific Ocean

Ring of Fire

Like a big round jigsaw puzzle, Earth's surface is broken up into about a dozen large pieces, called plates. More than half of the world's approximately 1,400 active volcanoes (some shown here with red triangles) are found along the edges of the large Pacific plate, which is bounded by subduction zones on most sides. This circle of intense volcanic activity is known as the "Ring of Fire."

Let's Compare

Volcanoes on Other Worlds

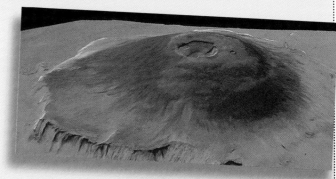

Volcanoes on other planets differ from Earth's. Mars, for example, has volcanoes much larger than Earth's, because Mars seems to lack tectonic plates. On Earth, a plate's movement tends to carry a volcano away from the magma source below. One Martian cone, Olympus Mons, may have erupted for a billion years; it's more than three times the height of Earth's Mount Everest.

Olympus Mons on Mars *(above)*, the Solar System's biggest volcano, measures a towering 29 km (18 mi.) high and 600 km (372 mi.) across.

A volcano shoots liquid sulfur *(right)* 298 km (185 mi.) above the surface of Io, one of Jupiter's 16 moons.

Volcanoes on Venus *(right)* paved most of the surface with lava, then became extinct about 500 million years ago.

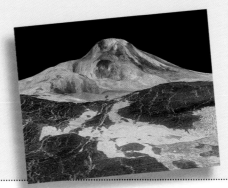

What Comes out of a Volcano?

Lava sometimes shoots out of a volcano in a fantastic display like fireworks. But **lava** can also ooze—slowly or quickly, depending on how much silica is in it. (Silica is the main ingredient in sand.) Fluid, silica-poor lava can form a glowing red-hot river that spreads for many miles before cooling and hardening. Lava that has more silica creeps along as a gooey, sticky mass like tar.

Lava flows can destroy homes and other objects, but most flows move so slowly that people can walk away from them. Rarely, waves of lava have rushed downhill at 100 km/h (60 mph).

Far deadlier are volcanic explosions, especially those that create hot, fast-moving **pyroclastic flows** of ash, gas, and rock. Some very ferocious volcanoes have shot ash more than 40 km (25 mi.) up into the sky, at twice the speed of sound. Powerful ash eruptions can change Earth's weather. Ash and sulfur gases thrown high into the atmosphere travel around the planet, blocking sunlight and lowering temperatures.

Types of Lava Flows

AA LAVA

Aa (pronounced "ah-ah") lava flows move sluggishly and form sharp, jagged surfaces that are difficult and dangerous to walk on when cool. An aa flow can pile up in a blanket 100 m (328 ft.) thick.

PAHOEHOE LAVA

Pahoehoe (pronounced "pahoy-hoy") flows are hotter, thinner, and faster moving than aa flows, and are rarely more than 1 m (3 ft.) thick. As the lava cools, it forms a thin, flexible skin, which folds into ropelike coils.

PILLOW LAVA

Pillow lava forms on the ocean floor or at the ocean's edge, where oozing or gently flowing lava cools quickly in cold seawater.

Volcanic smoke and dust particles can cause lightning inside the ash cloud of an erupting volcano. In this explosive eruption of Sakurajima *(left)*, in Japan, the smoke and dust particles rushed upward at 145 km/h (90 mph). Friction between these moving particles and the air around the cloud produced charges of static electricity, just as rubbing your feet on a carpet and then touching a doorknob produces a spark of electricity. The result was these violent lightning flashes inside the cloud.

Mt. Pinatubo

In June 1991, Mount Pinatubo in the Philippines erupted. Its huge, thick clouds of ash blocked the sunlight, leaving nearby farms and villages, like the one shown here, in total darkness for the next three days. Then the ash slowly settled, burying fields and homes for miles around. Warned by scientists that the volcano was about to explode, more than 250,000 people evacuated to a safer area, but 800 others stayed behind—and died.

Lava Bombs

Lava bombs are solidified blobs of **magma**. Hurled from volcanoes as molten rock, they cool in midair and land on Earth's surface as solid rock. They can take on many different shapes as they spin through the air, although most are rounded. Some bombs are as big as a house, others as small as a golf ball.

Above, a motorist pauses between two large lava bombs that were thrown out of Mount Teide on Tenerife, in the Canary Islands, sometime in the 19th century.

Would You Believe?

Ash Basketball

A thick, fresh layer of volcanic ash can turn into a devastating landslide or mud slide.

When heavy rains soak the fallen ash, a giant mudflow can race down the mountain and bury trees, roads, bridges, houses—everything in its path. Then the mud dries hard, like concrete. Here, boys play on a hardened volcanic mudflow that almost completely buried a basketball court after the 1980 eruption of Mount St. Helens.

Mount St. Helens

Mount St. Helens, in Washington State, was a sleeping giant—it had not erupted since 1857—but in the spring of 1980 it began to wake up. On March 27, steam exploded from the summit, opening a small crater. By April 8, the crater was 500 m (1,700 ft.) wide and 250 m (850 ft.) deep. Most menacing of all, the north side of the mountain developed a rocky bulge—caused by the upward pressure from a rising **magma** chamber—that grew 1.5 m (5 ft.) a day.

Then, on the clear and calm Sunday morning of May 18, an earthquake broke loose the bulging north slope of the mountain and sent it sliding downhill. No longer under pressure, superheated water that had been trapped in rock or magma flashed to steam. Gases, too, were suddenly free to expand; as a result, Mount St. Helens exploded with the fury of 500 atomic bombs.

As blasts ripped apart the mountain's north face, they hurled out rocks and chunks of ice the size of school buses. An avalanche of stony debris was overtaken by a wave of scalding-hot gases and choking ash. Although 198 people were rescued from the 600-square-km (232-sq.-mi.) blast zone, 61 did not get out in time.

8:32:47.0

8:32:53.2

8:33:02.3

At 8:32 a.m. on May 18, 1980, an earthquake triggered a landslide *(top)* on Mount St. Helens. Ash, steam, and gases spurt from cracks at the top and on the north side *(center)*. In 10 more seconds, the landslide opened the magma reservoir *(bottom)*. The eruption at full blast is at right.

Let's Compare

A volcanic pipsqueak when compared with blasts from the past, Mount St. Helens belched out only a single cubic kilometer of pumice and ash. That is about 100 times less than one of history's biggest eruptions in 1815, when Indonesia's Mount Tambora killed 12,000 people outright and another 80,000 by starvation and disease.

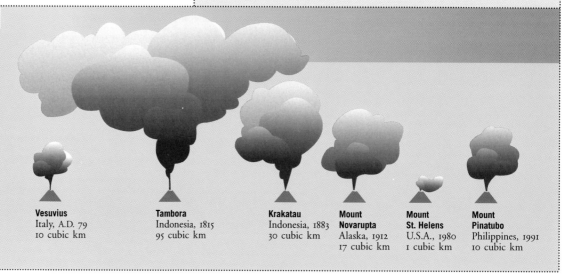

Vesuvius
Italy, A.D. 79
10 cubic km

Tambora
Indonesia, 1815
95 cubic km

Krakatau
Indonesia, 1883
30 cubic km

Mount Novarupta
Alaska, 1912
17 cubic km

Mount St. Helens
U.S.A., 1980
1 cubic km

Mount Pinatubo
Philippines, 1991
10 cubic km

A Mountain
Blows Its Top

May 18, 1980

Mount St. Helens Close up

Before
APRIL 1980

Mount St. Helens delivered a triple whammy to the forested wilderness to its north. Most areas were hit first by a billowing cloud of rock, ash, steam, and hot gases. This cloud was heated to 260°C (500°F), and it charged downhill at 1,078 km/h (670 mph). Trees within 4.8 km (3 mi.) of the summit vanished—vaporized or hurled through the air to places unknown.

The second punch was an avalanche of debris—mainly mud, ash, rock, and ice. Moving 250 to 290 km/h (155 to 180 mph), this landslide sloshed the water out of Spirit Lake as if from a bathtub.

After
SEPTEMBER 1980

Harry Truman

Harry Truman, 84 years old, ran the Mount St. Helens Lodge on the shores of Spirit Lake. He had lived at the foot of the volcano for more than 50 years. When sheriff's deputies warned

Mudflows, created when hot ash melted the ice blocks that had tumbled from the mountaintop, were the third and final blow. The ooze raced down riverbeds at 48 km/h (30 mph), pulverizing bridges, swallowing homes, and killing animals.

him that the mountain would blow, he refused to leave.

"I'm going to stay right here," said the outspoken old gentleman. "I am part of that mountain. It's a part of me."

Surrounded by his 16 cats, Harry Truman stubbornly settled into his cozy lodge. He had stored some food and supplies in a nearby mine shaft, hoping to hole up there when the mountain exploded. He probably never made it.

When the mountain erupted on May 18, there was little warning. The lodge at Spirit Lake quickly disappeared under 12 m (40 ft.) of ash and mud. Harry Truman's body was never found.

"Nothing was left. It's like a huge vacuum just sucked everything out of there."

A logger who visited Mount St. Helens four months after the deadly eruption.

Pompeii, A.D. 79   Vesuvius Erupts!

When Vesuvius erupted in A.D. 79, it destroyed the southern Italian city of Pompeii—but saved it forever. Ninety percent of the city's population got out in time, but 2,000 people refused to leave. Lightweight, porous rocks called pumice (some the size of rice grains, others the size of a fist) rained down on the streets and piled up at the astounding rate of 15 cm (6 in.) per hour. Then Vesuvius sent a scalding **pyroclastic flow** *(pages 34-35)*—a cloud of ash, gas, and rock—surging down the mountain. No one remaining in Pompeii survived this choking hot avalanche.

Within 19 hours, Pompeii lay buried beneath a layer of debris 8 m (25 ft.) thick. The ash hardened in place, saving every detail of daily life. The buried city was untouched for more than 1,700 years. Then in 1863 archaeologists began digging out Pompeii.

Much of what we know about this eruption comes from a letter, part of which is below, written by Pliny the Younger to the Roman historian Tacitus, describing what he saw that fateful day.

I Was There!

Pliny the Younger

"A dense, black cloud was coming up behind us, spreading over the earth like a flood. Darkness fell as if the lamp had been put out in a closed room. The buildings were shaking as if they were being torn from their foundations. Ashes were falling hotter and thicker, followed by bits of pumice and blackened stones, charred and cracked by the flames. You could hear the shrieks of women, and the wailing of infants and the shouting of men. I had the belief that the whole world was dying and I with it until a yellowish sun finally revealed a landscape buried deep in ashes like snowdrifts."

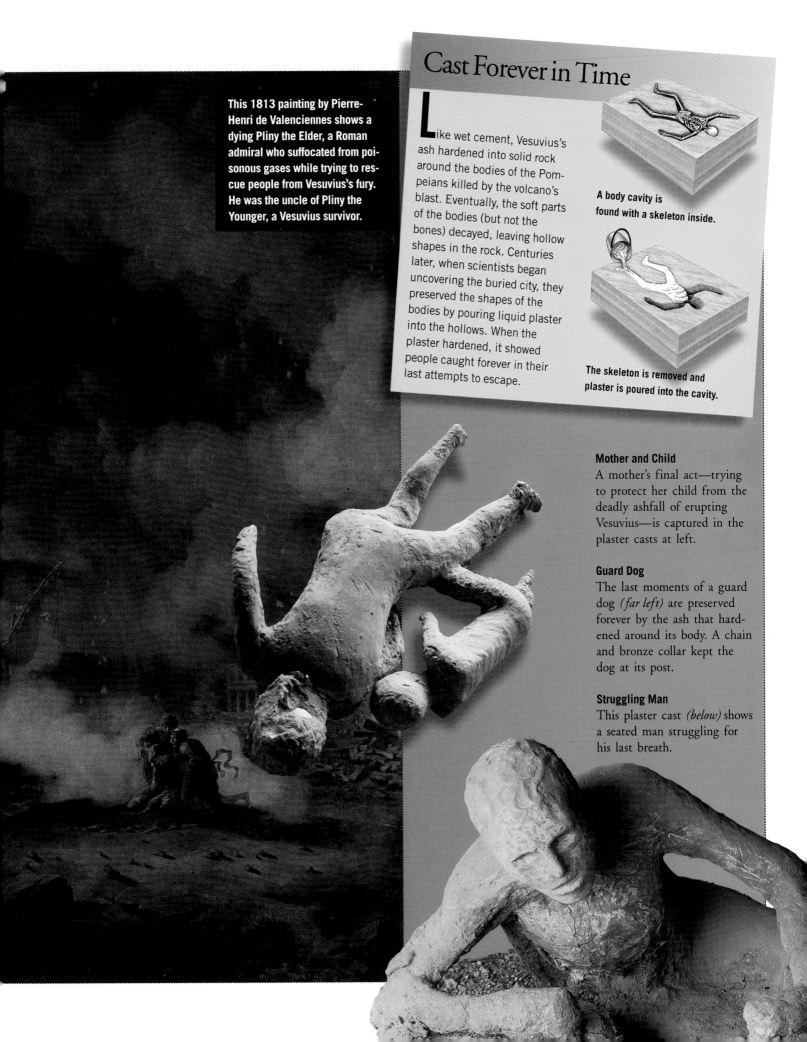

This 1813 painting by Pierre-Henri de Valenciennes shows a dying Pliny the Elder, a Roman admiral who suffocated from poisonous gases while trying to rescue people from Vesuvius's fury. He was the uncle of Pliny the Younger, a Vesuvius survivor.

Cast Forever in Time

Like wet cement, Vesuvius's ash hardened into solid rock around the bodies of the Pompeians killed by the volcano's blast. Eventually, the soft parts of the bodies (but not the bones) decayed, leaving hollow shapes in the rock. Centuries later, when scientists began uncovering the buried city, they preserved the shapes of the bodies by pouring liquid plaster into the hollows. When the plaster hardened, it showed people caught forever in their last attempts to escape.

A body cavity is found with a skeleton inside.

The skeleton is removed and plaster is poured into the cavity.

Mother and Child
A mother's final act—trying to protect her child from the deadly ashfall of erupting Vesuvius—is captured in the plaster casts at left.

Guard Dog
The last moments of a guard dog *(far left)* are preserved forever by the ash that hardened around its body. A chain and bronze collar kept the dog at its post.

Struggling Man
This plaster cast *(below)* shows a seated man struggling for his last breath.

Living with Volcanoes

magine living near a volcano that regularly spits out ash or **lava.** Many people around the world live dangerously close to an active or potentially active volcano. Scientists study these volcanoes carefully, trying to predict how they might act. But scientific predictions can't always save people from a volcanic disaster. Each year, about 50 volcanoes erupt on land, causing hundreds to die and thousands to flee their homes.

Although volcanoes can be very destructive, they can also do good. The ash from volcanoes fertilizes soil, making plants grow bigger and healthier. And heat from the **magma** of some volcanoes turns water into steam, which is then harnessed in geothermal ("earth-heated") plants to make electricity. In Iceland, a country with many volcanoes, magma-heated steam provides electricity for almost half of the homes.

Strange But TRUE!

Right in Their Own Backyard

On the afternoon of February 20, 1943, Mexican farmer Dionisio Pulido heard his cornfield growl. As he and his son ran to safety, smoke, ash, and glowing stones shot from a crack in the ground. As they watched, the volcano, Paricutín (below), was born. In a year it grew to 336 m (1,102 ft.) and erased the homes of 2,628 people.

Being a volcanologist—a scientist who studies volcanoes—is a really hot job. Volcanologists spend much of their time in laboratories analyzing rock, ash, and gas samples. They also make field trips to active volcanoes, where they collect these samples and make other measurements and observations. When near an active volcano's crater, volcanologists wear protective clothing, like the suit at left. It has a metal coating that reflects heat, thus keeping the scientist inside cool. Because volcanoes are so unpredictable, many volcanologists have died while doing their work.

Icelanders bathe in the warm magma-heated waters *(above)* at a geothermal electric plant near Reykjavík, Iceland.

All 5,000 residents of Vestmannaeyjar, Iceland, had to evacuate their homes in 1973 when a volcano suddenly cracked open the earth and erupted on the edge of town *(left)*. Many homes, including these, gradually disappeared beneath a blanket of black ash.

Heads Up!

Japanese students living at the foot of Sakurajima, one of the world's most active volcanoes, are required to wear hard hats when outdoors for protection from small lava bombs.

What Is an Earthquake?

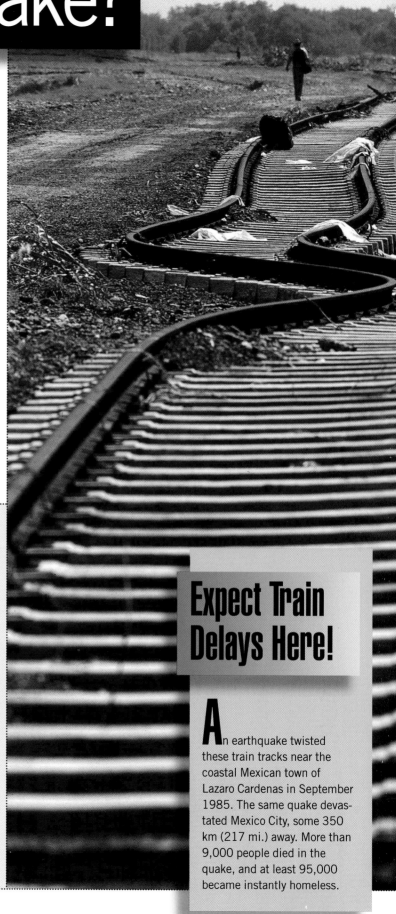

Have you ever stretched a rubber band so far that it snapped in two? A similar kind of action happens during an earthquake. Earth's **tectonic plates** *(pages* 14-15*)* are constantly colliding and grinding against each other. This puts a great stress on the rocks in Earth's upper crust. These rocks can absorb some of the stress elastically, like a rubber band. But if the stress becomes too great, the rocks will break and snap back to their original shape—just like the rubber band. The breaking of the rock unleashes the ground-shaking vibrations that we call an earthquake.

More than a million earthquakes rattle Earth each year. Fortunately, most are too small to cause damage or even for people to notice. But a few (about 20 or so) strike with devastating—and deadly—strength. In a 1976 earthquake that jolted the northern Chinese city of Tangshan, for example, more than 242,000 people died. It was one of the deadliest earthquakes in history.

A Fishy Explanation

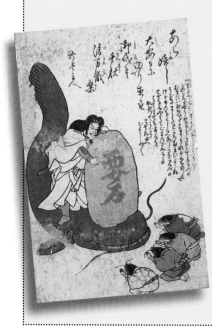

Long ago, people did not know the scientific explanation for earthquakes. So they made up stories to account for these frightful ground rumblings. The Japanese thought earthquakes were caused by the namazu, a giant catfish who lived deep within Earth. It was up to the warrior Kashima to hold the namazu down with a large rock *(left).* But sometimes Kashima let down his guard, and the namazu thrashed about, shaking the ground above.

Expect Train Delays Here!

An earthquake twisted these train tracks near the coastal Mexican town of Lazaro Cardenas in September 1985. The same quake devastated Mexico City, some 350 km (217 mi.) away. More than 9,000 people died in the quake, and at least 95,000 became instantly homeless.

Anatomy of an Earthquake

Most earthquakes take place along the boundary, or fault, between two tectonic plates. The strain of the plates' motions against one another causes rocks along the fault to break. The place deep in the Earth where the rocks break is known as the quake's hypocenter. The energy released by the breaking rocks causes shock waves, known as seismic waves, to ripple through Earth and over its surface. The waves are what cause the ground to rumble. The strongest waves are felt at the quake's epicenter, the point on the ground directly above the hypocenter.

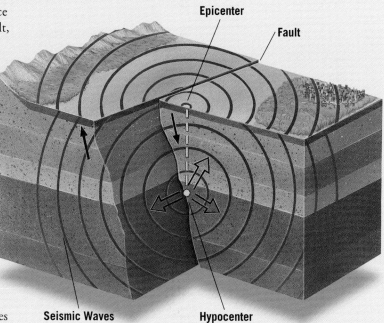

Epicenter

Fault

Seismic Waves

Hypocenter

Earthquake Risk

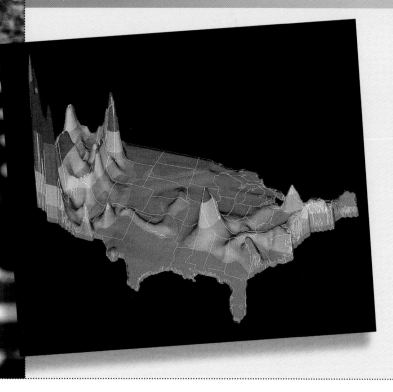

Many people in the United States think only the country's western states—especially California—are at risk of having an earthquake. But as this computer-drawn map shows, the potential for damaging earthquakes is also high in some eastern areas. The map uses color and relief to illustrate where earthquakes are most likely to occur in the United States. Relatively low-risk areas are flat and colored dark green; red peaks show the places where earthquakes are most likely to happen.

Measuring an Earthquake

H ow big was it? That's one of the first things people—including scientists—want to know when they learn an earthquake has struck somewhere in the world. Scientists measure the strength, or magnitude, of an earthquake with a seismograph, a device that detects and records the quake's seismic waves. They use several scales to describe the strength of an earthquake.

The best-known one is the Richter scale, named after its American inventor, Charles Richter. It ranks quakes on a scale of 0 to 9. (The scale goes higher, but no quake has measured stronger than an 8.9 since the 1930s, when the scale was first used.) On the Richter scale, an earthquake of 2.0 or 3.0 is very weak, while one that measures 8.0 can be truly devastating. An 8.0 quake releases 1 million times as much energy as a 2.0 quake.

Seismographs

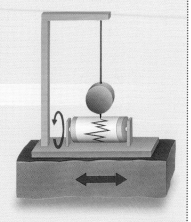

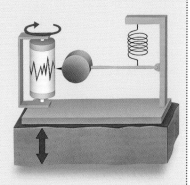

The two basic kinds of seismographs (tremor-recording device) record either horizontal motion *(right, top)*, or vertical motion *(right, bottom)*. Each has a frame and a weight hung on a wire or spring. When the ground shakes, the weight stays still but the frame vibrates, so that a pen at the end of the weight traces a zigzag pattern on a roll of paper. From such jagged tracings, or seismograms, scientists can tell when and where an earthquake took place.

Traveling Shock Waves

PRIMARY WAVES

The fastest seismic waves from an earthquake are called primary waves. They stretch and compress Earth's crust as they move through it.

SURFACE WAVES

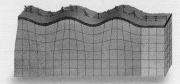

The waves that move along the surface are the most destructive. They can cause Earth's surface to whip side to side *(right, above)* or roll up and down *(right, below)* like ocean waves in a storm.

Would You Believe?

Telltale Toads

I n A.D. 132, the Chinese scientist Chang Heng invented the first instrument for recording earthquakes. The device shown here is a model of the original, which was about 2 m (6 ft.) across. It was ringed with 12 dragons and 12 toads. The dragons held bronze balls in their jaws. During a tremor, one of the dragons would drop the ball with a warning clank into the mouth of the toad below. The device also showed the direction of the quake; the toad farthest from the epicenter caught the ball.

How **Big?**

The Richter Scale

Magnitude 1-2

The earthquake can be detected only by seismographs or other instruments. More than 500,000 quakes of this magnitude happen each year.

Magnitude 3-4

The earthquake can just barely be felt. Hanging lights may swing; few things get damaged. Between 10,000 and 100,000 of these quakes happen each year.

Magnitude 5-6

The earthquake can be felt very strongly. Objects fall off shelves and walls crack. Between 20 and 200 of these quakes occur each year.

Magnitude 7-8

The quake causes tremendous damage. Buildings and bridges collapse. Roads buckle. As many as 10 of these big quakes happen each year.

Residents of Fukui, Japan, dodge cracks in the street as they flee a 1948 earthquake. The quake, which measured 7.3 on the Richter scale, killed 3,500 people. Most of them died in the fires that swept through the city after the quake.

I Was There!

Magazine photographer Carl Mydans (right), who took the terror-filled photograph above, was dining in a restaurant when the first tremors of the 1948 Fukui earthquake hit. He described what happened:

"The concrete floor just exploded. Tables and dishes flew into our faces and we were all hurled into a mad dance, bouncing about like popping corn. When at last I got near the doorway, I hurled myself at it. But the floor shifted, and I smashed into the crumbling wall a yard farther along."

51

San Francisco, 1906

One of the most famous earthquakes in history took place in San Francisco on April 18, 1906. The first tremor came at 5:12 a.m., while most people were still sleeping. It lasted only about 40 seconds but was soon followed by another shock, which rattled the ground for a minute and a half. Thousands of buildings collapsed as terrified residents ran into the streets. But that was only the start of the disaster. Fires soon broke out and spread quickly across the city. Firefighters could do little to stop the raging flames, for the city's water mains had burst.

The fires burned on for three horror-filled days. At the end of the long ordeal, 315 people had died and another 352 were missing. More than 30,000 of San Francisco's buildings were destroyed, leaving 250,000 men, women, and children homeless.

Thousands of San Franciscans return to the city's center to see the still-smoldering buildings where they once lived and worked (above).

California's Faults

San Francisco

San Andreas Fault

California straddles two gigantic **tectonic plates,** the Pacific and the North American. The grinding movement of these plates has created a network of faults (red lines at left) in Earth's crust. The most famous is the San Andreas fault, 1,100 km (682 mi.) long. San Francisco sits beside this fault.

I Was There!

"The moment I felt the house tremble . . . I leaped out of bed and rushed out to the front door. . . . I was sure the house would fall before I got out. It rocked, like a ship on 'rough sea.' Streams of people . . . poured into the streets . . . a mourning, groaning, sobbing, wailing, weeping, and praying crowd. The deathly-still air [was] very oppressive . . . quiver after quiver followed . . . until it seemed as if the very heart of this old earth was broken and was throbbing and dying away slowly and gently.

"Then the awful fires broke out . . . & no water to speak of. . . . There was no way to fight the fire except to dynamite the buildings. . . .

"Night came on, but there was no night for us. The reflection of the fire extended over the city changing night into day. . . ."

—From a letter by Exa Atkins Campbell, a young woman who survived the 1906 quake.

Deadly Inferno

Soldiers walk a burned-out street to keep away looters. One of the blazes that gutted San Francisco after the earthquake was accidentally started by a woman cooking a breakfast of ham and eggs. By feeding her family their usual meal, she had hoped to make the shattered world around them seem normal again.

Modern San Francisco

Buildings constructed today in San Francisco must be earthquake resistant, like the pyramid-shaped Transamerica Pyramid at left. It is designed to sway only 0.6 m (2 ft.) during a quake, compared to 0.9 m (3 ft.) for a normal building of the same height.

Kobe, 1995

On January 17, 1995, the people of Kobe, Japan, woke to a disaster. Their historic port city was being shaken by a massive earthquake—one that quickly registered 7.2 on the Richter scale. That dreadful tremor lasted less than a minute. Within those few seconds, homes crumbled, bridges toppled, roads buckled. Two 29,500-kg (65,000-lb.) cars from a passenger train were tossed like toys onto the roof of a nearby train terminal.

The Kobe quake killed 5,500 people and injured thousands more. More than 190,000 buildings were damaged or destroyed. Many homes burned to the ground when gas lines broke and sparks ignited the gas, or when kitchen items fell on hot kerosene stoves. Fires raged for two days. Still, the Kobe quake was not the worst earthquake to hit Japan in the 20th century. That awful event was the Great Kanto Earthquake of 1923, which killed 143,000 people in Tokyo and nearby towns.

Where the Fault Lies

Japan has many earthquakes because it sits at the intersection of four **tectonic plates** *(right)*. Of these, the Pacific plate is the fastest moving; it is **subducting**, or descending, beneath the Eurasian plate at a rate of 10 cm (4 in.) a year. The Kobe quake began when rock in the Eurasian plate's crust broke to relieve the strain caused by the Pacific plate's movement under it. The place where the rock snapped—the hypocenter of the quake—was 15 to 20 miles southeast of Kobe, along the Nojima fault.

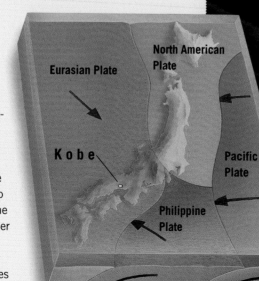

Eurasian Plate

North American Plate

Kobe

Pacific Plate

Philippine Plate

Awesome Power!

The powerful Kobe quake buckled much of the track for the city's trains. This train station suffered massive damage during the terrible tremor.

Roadway Collapse

The Kobe earthquake caused a 1 km (0.6 mi.) section of the Hanshin Expressway, an elevated highway, to tilt over on its side. Cars and trucks tumbled over as well.

Fast FACTS

The Heaviest Hitters

Scientists sometimes describe the strength of an earthquake by how many people it kills. Quakes that strike near large cities can be particularly deadly. The following earthquakes were some of the deadliest in history.

Country	Year	Deaths
India	1737	300,000
Turkey	115	260,000
China	1976	242,000
Syria	1139	230,000
Iran	1780	200,000
Japan	1923	143,000
Italy	1908	110,000
Indonesia	1883	100,000

Kobe scenes

Photographs taken after the quake show how much damage it caused. A bus dangles off a broken section of the Hanshin Expressway *(right, top).* In the Nagata Ward, one of the hardest-hit areas of the city, bits and pieces of collapsed buildings litter the street *(right, center).* And a rubber factory, which once made most of Japan's rubber boots, lies in ruins *(right, bottom).*

What Are Rocks?

Rocks are clumps of **minerals** and other solid material. Some kinds of rocks include organic matter, such as fossilized plants. Rocks seem permanent—have you ever used the expression "solid as a rock"?—but in fact, they change and move constantly. As they do, they spread minerals through Earth's crust in a never-ending process called the **rock cycle**.

Geologists group rocks into three types: **igneous**, **sedimentary**, or **metamorphic**. Rock melted to **magma** by the heat within Earth, then cooled, is igneous. **Weathering** at Earth's surface gradually breaks rock down to pieces. Carried to the seafloor by rivers, then buried, the pieces become cemented together into sedimentary rock.

As the huge rock plates in Earth's crust move, they can press against or beneath each other. The heat and intense pressure that build up gradually change igneous and sedimentary rock to metamorphic rock.

Ayers Rock

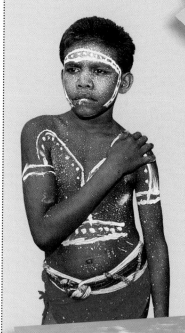

The *Guinness Book of World Records* lists Ayers Rock, in Australia, as the biggest rock in the world. (Actually, geologists consider it a rock formation rather than a rock.) It is a piece of sandstone 2.4 km (1.5 mi.) long, 1.6 km (1 mi) wide, and 348 m. (1,143 feet) high. Ayers Rock is sacred to Aborigines such as the boy at left, dressed for a traditional ritual.

The Rock Cycle

Weathering breaks rock down into smaller pieces. These pieces wash into the sea and become buried. Newer layers press down on the loose pieces, eventually changing them into sedimentary rock.

Deep inside Earth, intense heat melts rock to liquid magma. Pushed into cracks, or out a volcano, magma cools to become igneous rock.

As a continental plate rises, metamorphic rock may be exposed at the surface. Not all rocks complete a full cycle.

Where continental and oceanic plates meet, the heavier oceanic plate burrows under. It carries sedimentary and igneous rock deep down into the crust to become metamorphic rock. If hot enough, the rock may melt into magma and re-cool as igneous rock.

Types of Rocks

Igneous
Granite, Yosemite National Park, California

Granite

Granite forms when magma cools slowly underground. As the rock above it erodes, the granite eventually shows up on the surface. At Mount Rushmore in South Dakota, a granite cliff has been carved into busts of American presidents.

Sedimentary
Navajo sandstone, Utah

Sandstone

Sandstone is a sedimentary rock. It is made of compressed sand particles. Some sandstone is eroded by wind into beautiful natural shapes. Ancient Egyptians carved the Great Sphinx from sandstone some 4,000 years ago.

Metamorphic
Marble quarry near Carrara, Italy

Marble

When rock is heated and squeezed with tremendous pressure, it can change, or metamorphose, into another kind of rock. **Marble** began as limestone, a sedimentary rock, but then changed into metamorphic rock. A prince in India built his wife's tomb, the Taj Mahal, from marble.

What Is a Mineral?

Minerals Combine as Rock

Mineral is the name given to certain kinds of solid substances in nature. If you've ever seen shiny flecks of mica in a rock, you've seen a **mineral**. Minerals are inorganic—that is, they don't have any plant or animal material. Rocks themselves are not minerals, but they are usually made of one or more minerals. There are some 2,000 known minerals on earth, each with its own distinctive structure and chemical makeup. Geologists can identify them by studying properties such as hardness, crystal structure, and cleavage (how they break).

Minerals are made of one or more chemical elements. **Elements** are pure substances made from only one kind of atom. In a mineral, the atoms are arranged in repeating patterns that form **crystals.** Sometimes minerals are formed quickly, as when water evaporates, leaving behind the mineral salt. However, most minerals, and especially the more valuable ones such as diamonds and emeralds, form gradually over millions of years as they slowly cool while rocks press down on them from above.

Granite

If you look closely at **granite**, you can see the three minerals from which it is commonly made: **quartz,** mica, and feldspar. Granite is an igneous rock. It forms when a certain type of **magma** cools slowly underground, allowing large crystals to grow. The crystals lock tightly together, giving granite strength and its handsome, flecked look.

Quartz

Mica

Feldspar

From Atoms to Rock

Atom
A tiny, invisible particle; the basic building block of matter

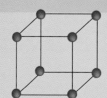

Element
A material made up of all the same kind of atom

Mineral
One or more elements arranged in a characteristic crystalline structure

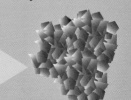

Rock
One or more minerals cemented together; a rock can contain pieces of other rocks

Common Table Salt

Take sodium—an element that is explosive in water. Crystallize it with equal parts of chlorine—a poisonous gas used to kill soldiers in World War I. Sprinkle the crystals on your food and taste it. Does the food explode? Is it poisonous? No. It is salty. When explosive sodium and poisonous chlorine crystallize together, they form the mineral halite, more commonly known as salt.

Halite Crystal

Magnetic Minerals

Ancient sailors used compasses that contained a chunk of a mineral with magnetic properties. They called the chunk a lodestone. Today we know that mineral as magnetite, a form of iron oxide.

Where large formations of magnetite occur in Earth's crust, compass needles will swerve away from Earth's magnetic north pole to point to the magnetite. There have even been reported cases of airplanes getting lost when their compass needle pointed to magnetite on the ground below.

Everyday Minerals

From the time you pick up your steel breakfast spoon in the morning to the time you put away your graphite pencil at night, you use minerals over and over again. Of the 2,000 or so minerals that have been identified by geologists, more than 75 are now in common use. About 34 of them, such as aluminum (for metals) and gypsum (for plaster), are used in large amounts.

The aluminum that goes into soda cans and airplanes is found mainly in a claylike substance called bauxite.

A light bulb contains a thread of tungsten that heats up and glows when an electrical current passes through it.

Aluminum
Used in power lines, cars, ships, planes, pots and pans, beverage cans.

Copper
Used in plumbing pipes, electrical wiring, roofing, coins.

Graphite
Used in pencils, lubricants.

Gypsum
Used in plaster and drywall.

Iron
Used in construction materials such as steel screws.

Lead
Used in electrical storage batteries and fishing weights.

Nickel
Used in aircraft and jet engine parts and in coins. (In fact, a nickel coin is almost pure nickel.)

Tungsten
Used in incandescent light bulbs.

Zinc
Used in metal to prevent rust.

Amazing Crystals

Crystal Shapes

L ook at a grain of table salt under a good magnifying glass. You'll see a tiny cube. Table salt is the **mineral** halite and, like all minerals, it has a distinctive structure. It is a **crystal.** There are six main crystal shapes *(right)*.

The word "crystal" comes from the Greek word "kryos," meaning frozen. Early Europeans thought that crystals such as **quartz** were simply ice, frozen so hard it could never be thawed. Most minerals form crystals with regular, well-defined faces, but not all crystals are minerals. Sugar, for example, forms crystals. But because sugar is made from plants—sugar beets or sugarcane—it is not considered a mineral.

All crystals have a precise internal structure, but on the outside their shape, size, and color can vary greatly. Most crystals form underground. There they compete for space with other minerals. As a result, they may have odd, irregular shapes. Size depends on how slowly and under what pressure crystals form. Slow growth makes bigger crystals. Color comes from chemical impurities. Rose quartz, for example, is tinted pink by titanium and iron.

Cubic
Fluorite *(far right)*, pyrite, diamond

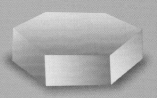

Hexagonal
Beryl *(far right)*, ice crystals, snowflakes

Monoclinic
Sphene *(far right)*, gypsum

Tetragonal
Wulfenite *(far right)*, zircon

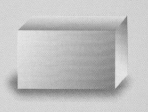

Orthorhombic
Andalusite *(far right)*, olivine, topaz

Triclinic
Amblygonite *(far right)*, plagioclase feldspars

Crystals of the gem tourmaline poke up out of a base of less precious minerals. Each crystal is about 15 cm. (6 in.) tall.

A flint ax head keeps the sharp edge that a Stone Age toolmaker gave it thousands of years ago. Because of its hardness, toolmakers still use flint—and other kinds of quartz—today.

Quartz: A Crystal for All Time

In 1880, Pierre and Jacques Curie (Marie Curie's husband and brother-in-law) discovered that quartz crystals have a property called piezoelectricity. Later scientists found that an alternating electrical current causes a quartz crystal to vibrate with astonishing regularity—30,000 times a second. Watchmakers of the 20th century put this property to use: Inside many watches a microthin quartz crystal keeps time.

S ilicon is a crystal that is made out of quartz in a laboratory. It forms the basis for almost all modern electronics. The wafer below holds hundreds of tiny silicon chips. Machines etch microscopic electrical circuits into the chips. Each chip can run a personal computer such as the laptop model at right.

What Are Gemstones?

Gemstones are jewels—**minerals** or stones that can be cut and polished for jewelry and other ornaments. Most gems are minerals. However, a handful of organic substances, such as pearls from oysters, amber from petrified sap, and ivory from elephant and walrus tusks, are also gems.

Three properties set gemstones apart from the pack: rarity, durability, and beauty. Only a very few minerals have what it takes to qualify. The most famous gemstones are sapphires, rubies, emeralds, and diamonds.

Gemstones don't all have the same value. Most diamonds *(pages 66-67),* for example, are of poor quality. Size, color, clarity, and brilliance are all important. Even reputation can add to a gem's value. A stone with a romantic past involving bloodshed and skullduggery will be worth more than one of equal size and beauty that doesn't possess an interesting story.

Amethyst **crystals** are exposed after a layer of rock has been removed. Cut and polished, they may turn into a sparkling gemstone like the oval jewel below. Although most gems crystallize deep within Earth, **erosion** can bring them near the surface. Over eons, the erosion can uncover deep layers of rock, including crystals that used to be kilometers deep.

Once gemstones are exposed, they can be washed into streambeds along with gravel and other sediments. Many rich gem-producing deposits, such as those in the famous sapphire-rich island of Sri Lanka, are simply ancient streambeds.

Crown Jewels

The Imperial State Crown *(right)* was made in 1937 for the coronation of King George VI of England. Today it is worn by his daughter, Queen Elizabeth II, at many official functions. This dazzling crown contains 2,868 diamonds, 17 sapphires, 11 emeralds, 5 rubies, and 273 pearls. The huge diamond up front is the Cullinan II, cut from the largest diamond ever mined. The large red stone, which is as big as a chicken egg, is known as the "Black Prince's Ruby," even though it is not a ruby. It is a spinel.

How Gems Form

Igneous Gems

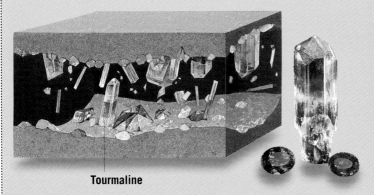

Tourmaline

When **granite**-forming **magma** forces its way into cracks in Earth's crust, the last part to become solid can produce gem-bearing rock pegmatites. These are igneous nurseries: Minerals dissolve from the rock above and then crystallize inside the spaces created by the pegmatites. Pegmatites can yield topaz, beryl (including emerald and aquamarine), and tourmaline *(left)*.

Sedimentary Gems

Rainwater

Silica

Opal

Opal is one of only a few gems formed during the process of sedimentation. As **groundwater** seeps downward, it may travel through layers of material, such as volcanic ash, that are rich in the compound silica. The water carries the silica down and drops it in crevices and cracks around rocks underground. The silica doesn't crystallize but forms masses of smooth, microscopic balls that form into shimmering opal *(left)*.

Carob beans—which come from the pod of the Mediterranean carob tree—are remarkably consistent in weight, all weighing about a fifth of a gram. Therefore, they were once used as a standard for comparing the weight of gems. Eventually the word "carob" was distorted to "carat," and the beans were replaced by standard weights of 200 mg (exactly ⅕ gram).

Metamorphic Gems

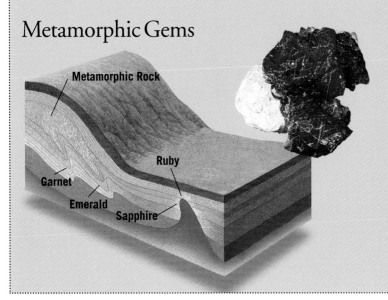

Metamorphic Rock

Ruby

Garnet

Emerald

Sapphire

When solid rock inside Earth heats almost to the melting point, minerals within it can change without melting. This metamorphism can occur in two ways. The first is when a tongue of magma intrudes into solid rock and heats the rock around it. A second way is compression. Moving plates of Earth's crust can squeeze rock so hard it heats to near melting. Gems produced in metamorphic rock include ruby *(left)*, sapphire, and garnet.

This enormous blue topaz owned by the Smithsonian Institution weighs a hefty 3,273 carats. That's almost ¾ kg (1½ lbs.).

Diamonds King of Minerals

There is perhaps no other substance on Earth with the romance and power of the diamond. It is one of the rarest gemstones and, because of its extreme hardness, the most enduring. But the life of a diamond is not all glitz and glamour. Diamonds too flawed for use in jewelry are still prized for their hardness. They may be used for such unexotic jobs as drilling teeth and sanding car doors.

Diamonds are among a handful of **minerals,** such as gold and copper, made of a single pure **element.** They are pure carbon, forged 96 to 152 km (60 to 95 mi.) deep within Earth under extreme heat and pressure, and they form only in a kind of rock called **kimberlite,** named for the South African mining town of Kimberley. Kimberlite forms in narrow, pipelike volcanic chimneys that are found on almost every continent.

Like many other gemstones, diamonds are also found in streambeds and ocean beaches. These gems have been washed down from eroded kimberlite pipes.

Diamond Mines

Miners 438 meters (1,400 ft.) below the surface at the Premier Mine in South Africa cut into rock with air-powered drills. Train cars haul the loosened rock to a crushing machine. Then the crushed pieces ride an elevator to the surface. Workers must sift through many tons of ore before they find a single diamond.

Where Are They Found?

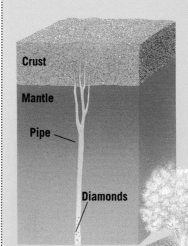

Diamonds form deep within the upper mantle, under Earth's crust, in narrow volcanic chimneys called kimberlite pipes. Intense heat and pressure from all sides cause diamond crystals to form from the **element** carbon.

Geologists believe **magma** explodes up through kimberlite pipes with shattering force. As it shoots its way through the crust to the surface, the magma carries diamonds with it.

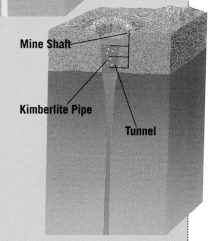

Kimberlite pipes are first mined where they reach the surface. Once rock has been dug down to about 312 m (1,000 ft.), danger from cave-ins forces miners to change tactics. They dig a deep shaft parallel to the kimberlite, then cut tunnels across to the pipe. Blasted loose, blue kimberlite rock is carried to the surface and sifted for diamonds.

Diamonds in the Rough

A sampler of rough—as in un-cut, unpolished—diamonds found in southern Africa shows a surprising range of shape and color. Colorless diamonds are usually the most valuable. The round, marble-like diamonds are ones that have been tumbled longest in streams or the sea.

A diamond—the hardest substance on Earth—and graphite in your pencil—one of the softest solids—are made of exactly the same ingredient: pure carbon. The difference lies in the structure of their crys-tals. In graphite, carbon atoms are arranged in layers that slide easily over one another. In a diamond, carbon atoms are arranged in a rigid, compact framework. Want to turn your pencil to diamond? Just apply pressure at 450,000 kg (1 million lbs.) per square inch and heat to 1,650°C (3,000°F.)

Strange But TRUE!

Hope Diamond

Legend has it that this blue dia-mond once was a 112-carat eye in a statue of the Hindu goddess Sita. When the stone was stolen, the story goes, the goddess promised bad luck to whoever used it. France's King Louis XIV wore it once, then died of small-pox. Louis XVI and Marie An-toinette wore it and died at the guillotine. Later owners suffered from other bad luck. The gem is named for one of its owners, Henry Thomas Hope. Today, it is on display at the Smithsonian Institution in Washington, D.C.

What Is Gold?

You might say gold is a magic mineral. It doesn't rust, tarnish, or corrode. It conducts heat and electricity. It is so flexible that a one-ounce nugget can be pulled into a wire 80 km (50 mi.) long or hammered into a thin, translucent sheet large enough to cover 10 square meters (108 sq. ft.). Its warm yellow color gives it great beauty. It is little wonder that gold has been one of the most widely sought minerals on Earth for thousands of years.

Prospectors searching for gold often look in streambeds. That's because of one of the chief properties of gold: its great density. Where rock bearing a vein of gold is exposed at the surface, weathering and **erosion** break away pieces of both. Rain washes them into streams. Because pieces of gold are so heavy, they tend to stop moving and collect wherever a stream slows down. Prospectors need only simple tools—and tedious hours of work—to extract this gold. There is more gold underground in gold-containing rock, called ore. But this kind of gold is more difficult and expensive to extract.

A weather-beaten prospector in the American West pans for gold in 1898. Such miners scraped gravel from riverbeds, then shook the pans. Lighter rock washed out. Heavy gold settled to the bottom of the pan.

Serra Palada

Goldminers swarm over a primitive open-pit mine in the rain forest of Brazil. Gold was discovered here in 1980 when a farmer spotted a particle of gold glittering in a stream. In a matter of days, hundreds of people arrived, staked out small claims, and began to carve into the ground for gold. The number of prospectors swelled to 22,000 within five weeks. Murder and mayhem were common until the government took control of the mine in 1983.

Gold Alchemy

For centuries, early chemists called alchemists sought to turn ordinary metal into gold. Virtually every king in medieval Europe employed an alchemist. It was not the safest of jobs—several kings, frustrated by failure, had their alchemists executed. An alchemist and his assistant are seen in this wood-cut created by German painter Hans Holbein in 1527.

All That Glitters Is Gold

A woman of the Adioukrou people of Africa's Côte d'Ivoire wears the family's wealth—a glittering display of gold jewelry—at a special ceremony. Gold dust glitters on her face and throat. From early times, gold has been made into jewelry and coins. In modern times, gold has new uses in electronics, medicine, and other technologies.

What's Fool's Gold?

Many a prospector's heart has been broken by this gold look-alike, the mineral pyrite. Pyrite and a similar-looking cousin called chalcopyrite are much harder than the real thing, and their color is not so pretty. Fool's gold is not always useless, however. Its presence in nature can be a clue that a vein of gold lies nearby.

Fossil Fuels

Turn on the oven, and you are burning fuel that comes from the partially decayed bodies of marine plants and animals some 300 million years old. Switch on a light, and you may be using energy yielded by the burning of swamp ferns from the Carboniferous period. Of course, those ferns and marine organisms have changed somewhat in 300 million years. Today, they are **coal** and **oil,** collectively known as **fossil fuels.**

Fossil fuels—oil, coal, and to a lesser extent natural gas—are the main fuels in the world today. Abundant, inexpensive coal fueled Britain's Industrial Revolution in the 19th century. It blackened the air above industrial cities with soot. Besides creating terrible air pollution, coal has other drawbacks. Coal mining can hurt the environment. Coal is also bulky and expensive to move. In the 1950s, the world began to switch over to petroleum oil.

Coal and oil are still forming beneath the ground. But, fossil fuels are not considered renewable resources. Because fossil fuels form over hundreds of millions of years, current supplies will be used up long before nature can replace them.

The Formation of Oil

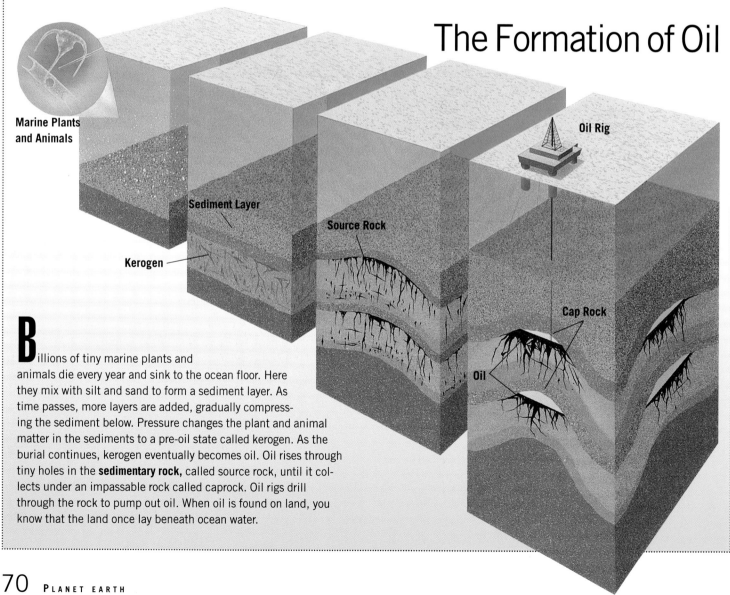

Marine Plants and Animals

Sediment Layer

Kerogen

Source Rock

Oil Rig

Cap Rock

Oil

Billions of tiny marine plants and animals die every year and sink to the ocean floor. Here they mix with silt and sand to form a sediment layer. As time passes, more layers are added, gradually compressing the sediment below. Pressure changes the plant and animal matter in the sediments to a pre-oil state called kerogen. As the burial continues, kerogen eventually becomes oil. Oil rises through tiny holes in the **sedimentary rock,** called source rock, until it collects under an impassable rock called caprock. Oil rigs drill through the rock to pump out oil. When oil is found on land, you know that the land once lay beneath ocean water.

The Formation of Coal

Peat

Coal begins forming when plants in and around a wetland die and build up under the water. Without much oxygen in the water, the plants decay just a little, turning into a spongy mass called peat.

Lignite

Layers of sand and silt gradually cover the peat. The heavy layers press down on the peat. They squeeze out much of the water and slowly change the peat into a burnable brown coal called lignite.

Bituminous Coal

As more layers press down on the lignite, it becomes bituminous coal, the most common type of coal used by coal-burning power plants. Bituminous coal may still contain some recognizable parts of plants.

Anthracite

As more sediment presses down on the coal layer, heat from below and pressure from above change it again. Bituminous coal turns to anthracite, the highest quality coal. Anthracite is cleaner when burned but expensive to mine.

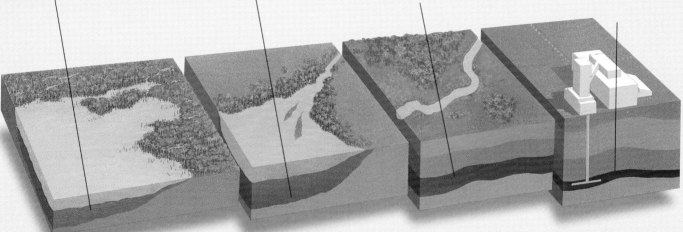

Coal Mining Kids

Deep in the dark underground passages of a coal mine, a young boy holds open a door for a mule pulling cars of coal. In the late 1800s and early 1900s, hard times sent thousands of boys as young as eight years old to work full days in the coal mines. Their families needed the money. Many boys died in cave-ins, explosions, and accidents involving train cars. The passage of child labor laws in the early 20th century brought the children back aboveground for good.

Sooty with coal dust, an 1890s Pennsylvania boy emerges from a hard day's work in the mines underground.

What Is the Ocean?

f you looked at Earth from a point in outer space right over the Pacific Ocean, the planet would look entirely blue. In fact, from any angle in space, Earth looks mostly blue. This is because more than two-thirds of its surface is covered by ocean waters. Geographers divide these waters into four separate oceans: the Atlantic, Pacific, Indian, and Arctic. Because all of these oceans are connected, they are sometimes called the World Ocean.

The ocean is in constant motion, driven largely by what's happening in the atmosphere above it. **Winds** blowing across its surface whip it into waves and drive its currents, which are vast meandering rivers that flow in the top layers of the ocean.

Beneath the ocean surface, temperature changes cause masses of water to rise and sink as if they were in a giant mixer. Because there is so much water in the ocean, it takes a long time to stir it all up. Bottom water may take 2,000 years to creep to the surface!

Let's Compare

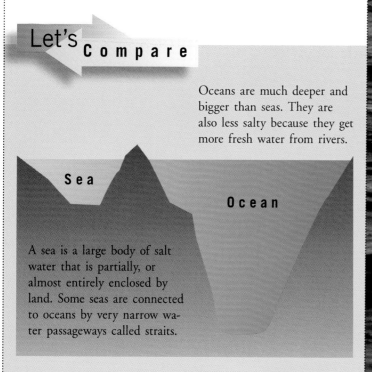

Oceans are much deeper and bigger than seas. They are also less salty because they get more fresh water from rivers.

Sea

Ocean

A sea is a large body of salt water that is partially, or almost entirely enclosed by land. Some seas are connected to oceans by very narrow water passageways called straits.

The World's Oceans

Arctic Ocean

Atlantic Ocean

Pacific Ocean

Pacific Ocean

Indian Ocean

What's in a Name?

Ocean

The word "ocean" comes from the Greek word "okeanos," which means "river." The ancient Greeks thought the ocean was one big saltwater river that flowed all the way around Earth.

How Big?

The world's largest ocean, the Pacific, has about 15 times more surface area than the smallest ocean, the Arctic, as shown in the diagram at right. But if you were to measure the total amount of water in both oceans, you would find that the deeper Pacific contains about 50 times more water than the Arctic.

Pacific Ocean
181,340,000 square km
(70,015,000 sq.mi.)

Atlantic Ocean
94,310,000 square km
(36,413,000 sq. mi.)

Indian Ocean
74,120,000 square km
(28,618,000 sq. mi.)

Arctic Ocean
12,260,000 square km
(4,734,000 sq. mi.)

Dolphins glide effortlessly through the waters of the Atlantic Ocean.

The Ocean Floor

If you could somehow drain the oceans, you would uncover a fantastic landscape of huge mountain ranges, deep valleys and trenches, and wide, flat plains that stretch on for hundreds of kilometers. You would also find more than 10,000 underwater volcanoes, many of them still active!

Until the 1920s, people thought the deep ocean floor was flat. That's when modern ships and equipment began to make it possible for scientists to accurately map the bottom of the ocean. By the 1950s, scientists had discovered a truly amazing feature: a huge interconnected mountain range that winds some 64,000 km (40,000 mi.) through all the world's oceans. This underwater range, made up of many oceanic ridges, is formed by hot melted rock, or **magma,** pushing up from Earth's **mantle.** Ridges are found at sites along the ocean floor where Earth's **tectonic plates** are slowly moving apart (*pages* 14-15). The ocean floor is growing larger, spreading outward from the ridges at the extremely slow pace of about 1 cm (0.39 in.) a year.

Mapping the Ocean Floor

Scientists can map the ocean floor from a ship towing a torpedo-shaped sonar device called GLORIA. GLORIA sends pulses of sound downward and sideways, in a swath up to 60 km (36 mi.) wide. The sound waves reflect off the ocean floor, and GLORIA records the time they take to return. The longer the time, the deeper the ocean is at that spot. Scientists collect hundreds of measurements and use computers to generate a map of the underwater mountains and valleys.

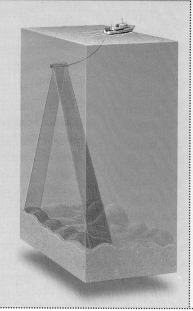

Continental Shelf

This gently sloping underwater extension of a continent is the shallowest part of the ocean. Most continental shelves were dry until the glaciers melted about 18,000 years ago.

Continental Slope

A continental shelf ends in an abrupt drop-off called a continental slope. Some are steeper than others.

Abyssal Plain

The flattest part of the ocean floor, an abyssal plain is one of the flattest areas on Earth—above or below water.

Realm of the Deep

Seamount

This is an underwater volcano. Some rise above the water to form islands.

Oceanic Ridge

An oceanic ridge is created when molten rock pushes up from deep inside Earth. Rising and spreading, the molten rock cools to form ridges in huge underwater mountain ranges. Ridges cover about one-third of the ocean floor.

Oceanic Trench

This is a great, steep, narrow canyon cut into the ocean floor. It marks a **subduction** zone, where the edge of one tectonic plate is going under another. Although found in every ocean, trenches cover only about 3 percent of the ocean floor.

How Deep?

The deepest part of the ocean is the Mariana Trench in the Pacific Ocean. The depth of this trench is greater by 1.6 km (1 mi.) than the height of Mount Everest, the world's highest mountain. And it is almost six miles deeper than Arizona's Grand Canyon.

Mariana Trench

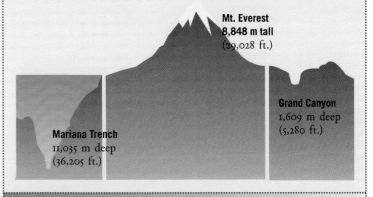

Mt. Everest 8,848 m tall (29,028 ft.)

Mariana Trench 11,035 m deep (36,205 ft.)

Grand Canyon 1,609 m deep (5,280 ft.)

Deep-Sea Life

On some oceanic ridges, vents called black smokers spew hot, mineral-rich waters *(right)* that support some surprising forms of life. Bacteria use hydrogen sulfide from the hot outflow to produce organic food molecules. Giant tubeworms *(below)* take this food in through their skin (they have no eyes, mouth, or intestine) and grow to be 1 m (3 ft.) long.

Currents & Tides

The surface waters of all the oceans contain great coiled rivers of horizontally moving water called currents. Global **winds** are the main force creating these currents. Earth's spin also affects their speed and direction.

Currents move through the oceans in large circular patterns called **gyres** (pronounced "jires"), at speeds from 16 to 161 km (10 to 100 mi.) a day. They move vast amounts of warm or cold water, and they have a big effect on global climate.

Ocean water also moves up and down along the shorelines in daily patterns called **tides**. Tides are caused by the gravitational and rotational forces of the Sun and Moon acting on Earth. Although the Sun is much larger than the Moon, it is also much farther away, so its pull on Earth's oceans is less than half as strong as the Moon's. Every ocean beach in the world experiences high tides and low tides daily. The difference between high tide and low tide—called the **tidal range**—varies from beach to beach, but is generally about 1 m (3 ft.). Tides also produce small, local currents, as the ocean covers and uncovers the beach.

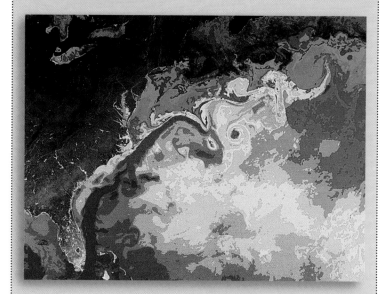

The **Gulf Stream** is one of the world's fastest-flowing ocean currents. It moves warm water from the Caribbean Sea northward along the eastern coast of the United States and across the Atlantic to Europe. Without the warming effect of the Gulf Stream, Britain and other areas of northern Europe would be much colder.

The Gulf Stream can travel at speeds of up to 160 km (100 mi.) a day. It carries 100 million cubic meters (3.5 billion cu. ft.) of water every second. That's 65 times more water than flows in all of the world's rivers combined.

World Currents

Ocean surface currents flow in five major gyres. These have been named the North Atlantic Gyre, the South Atlantic Gyre, the Indian Ocean Gyre, the North Pacific Gyre, and the South Pacific Gyre. Because of the way Earth spins, the gyres in the Northern Hemisphere flow in a clockwise direction, while those in the Southern Hemisphere flow counterclockwise.

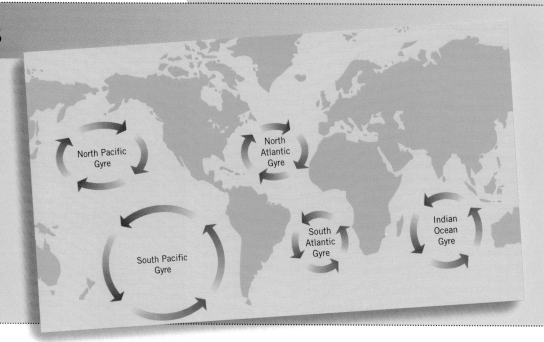

North Pacific Gyre

North Atlantic Gyre

South Pacific Gyre

South Atlantic Gyre

Indian Ocean Gyre

Norwegian Maelstrom

When surface currents and tidal currents collide, they can combine to form dangerous giant whirlpools, or **maelstroms,** in the ocean. Several of these whirlpools can be found off the coast of Norway. The whirling water's thundering roar can be heard up to 5 km (3 mi.) away.

The Tides

The Moon's "pull," or gravity, plays a big role in the ups and downs of Earth's tides. The Moon pulls most strongly on the ocean waters directly facing it *(right)*, creating a high tide. But the waters on Earth's far side also bulge outward, to form another high tide. This is because the Earth's and the Moon's movements through space create centrifugal force. This force pushes the ocean water away from Earth, much as water in a bucket pushes outward when you swing the bucket.

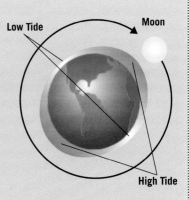

Low Tide Moon

High Tide

Steep banks and a narrow entranceway combine to give Canada's Bay of Fundy *(below)* one of the greatest tidal ranges in the world—almost 15 m (50 ft.)

HIGH TIDE

LOW TIDE

El Niño

Every two to 10 years, the waters of the Pacific Ocean act strangely. In response to changing wind patterns, the warm waters of the western tropical Pacific Ocean reverse their normal course and start flowing eastward, toward the continent of South America.

Sea levels drop in the western Pacific (along the east coasts of Australia and Asia) and rise in the east—sometimes by a third of a meter (1 ft.). The warm water reaching the coast of South America raises water temperatures there, sometimes by 4°C (7°F). These changes in the Pacific Ocean are the result of a powerful **weather** phenomenon known as **El Niño.**

The shifts in ocean **winds** and currents in the Pacific Ocean have been linked with catastrophic effects around the world, bringing heavy rains and floods to some areas and droughts and dust storms to others.

In late 1982 and early 1983, a particularly devastating El Niño killed more than 1,100 people around the world and destroyed property valued at 8.7 billion dollars. The pictures on these pages are scenes from that El Niño.

An El Niño occurs in any year when the prevailing easterlies (winds blowing from east to west) over the southern Pacific Ocean weaken. In normal years (*right, top*), the easterly winds push warm surface water away from the South American coast, making room for cooler waters to flow in. But in an El Niño year (*right, bottom*), these winds are so weak that winds from the west can push currents of warm water eastward.

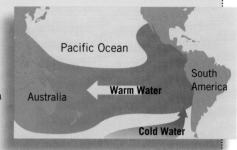

Normal Year

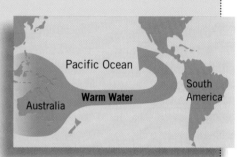

In an El Niño Year

Tahiti

Six freak **hurricanes** battered Tahiti and the neighboring islands of French Polynesia during five months in 1983. The island residents were taken completely by surprise because the last hurricane to hit them had occurred 75 years before! On Tahiti *(left),* water engulfed entire villages, leaving 25,000 people homeless. The storms destroyed some 1,500 houses and ripped the roofs from 6,000 others.

California

High **tides** and violent storms pounded the coastal towns of California in the summer and fall of 1982. Huge waves smashed seafront homes, while torrential rains washed away hillsides and flooded many towns such as Alviso *(above)*.

What's in a Name?

El Niño

El Niño is short for El Niño de Navidad, which means "the Christ Child" in Spanish. Fishermen along the coasts of Ecuador and Peru gave the phenomenon this name because it tends to appear in December, right around Christmastime.

Australia

The continent of Australia was probably the area hardest hit by the 1982-1983 El Niño. Rainfall ceased, and the severe drought *(above)* gave rise to blinding dust storms and raging bushfires *(left)*. All in all, this El Niño cost Australia a total of about 2.5 billion dollars.

What Are Waves?

From small, rolling ripples to huge, crashing white-caps, almost all ocean waves are caused by the same force: the **wind.** The longer and stronger the wind blows, the higher the waves. Wave size is also determined by the distance the wind travels over the water surface, known as the **fetch**. Waves are often tallest at the end of the wind's fetch.

The average ocean wave is about 1.5 to 3 m (5 to 10 ft.) high. During a typical storm, waves can crest at 21.3 m (70 ft.) or more. The biggest recorded storm wave reached a dizzying height of 45.7 m (150 ft.). It occurred off the coast of eastern Canada during a storm in 1991.

The most dangerous and deadliest of waves, however, is the **tsunami** (pronounced "tsoo-NAH-mee"). That's the Japanese word for "great harbor wave." Tsunamis are sometimes called tidal waves, but they have nothing to do with **tides,** nor are they caused by wind, like ordinary waves. Tsunamis are triggered by undersea earthquakes, volcanoes, or landslides. In deep water, a tsunami creates only a slight swell that ships pass over easily. Only when a tsunami reaches shore and crests—often at a height of more than 30.5 m (100 ft.)—does it threaten people and property.

How a Wave Works

Waves look as if they are moving water, but they are not. Water in a wave moves, but only up and down in a circular path. When water particles reach the top of their circular path, they form the crest, or top, of a wave. When the particles dip to the bottom of their path, they form the wave's trough. It's like a rope snapping. Waves wiggle down the rope, but the rope remains in the same place.

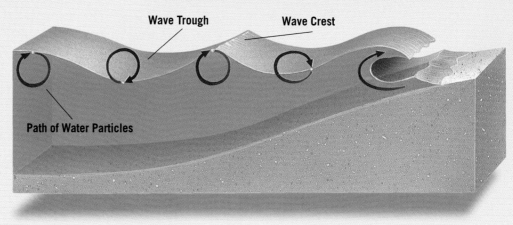

Wave Trough

Wave Crest

Path of Water Particles

A surfer catches a big one at Sunset Beach, Hawaii.

Tsunami's Destructive Power

How Tsunamis Occur

Most tsunamis are triggered by a sudden shift of the ocean floor during an undersea earthquake. The quake creates an enormous swell of water that breaks down into waves that race across the ocean at terrific speeds of up to 804 km/h (500 mph). In the photo below, residents of Hilo, Hawaii, flee for their lives as a tsunami crashes into their city on April 1, 1946. This tsunami was triggered by an earthquake off Alaska. It killed 159 people.

How **Far?**

Waves can travel for hundreds, even thousands, of miles, often only ending when they hit a shore. The large surfing waves that Hawaii is famous for actually start in storms 4,000 miles away off the Antarctic coast.

Hawaii

Antarctica

I Was There!

My mother [and I] were on the lawn picking flowers. Somebody yelled "tsunami!" . . . I looked up and saw a huge wall of dirty water. Palm trees 35 feet tall were covered by water. My mother pushed me inside and slammed the door, just as the wave struck our house. It felt like we'd been hit by a train. The wave picked up the house, and we floated away. . . . Through the windows we could see people floating by, holding onto whatever they could. A boy was clinging to a piece of lumber. . . . Finally our house slammed into a factory wall. Somehow my parents and I climbed into the factory, where we found some neighbors on the upper floor. We all got busy tearing burlap sugar bags into strips to make a rope. Whenever someone floated by, we threw them the rope.

—Mieko Browne, who was 18 years old in 1946 when a tsunami struck her home in Hilo, Hawaii.

Exploring the Ocean

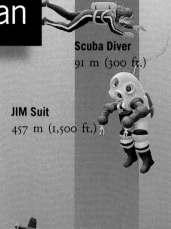

Scuba Diver
91 m (300 ft.)

JIM Suit
457 m (1,500 ft.)

Exploring the ocean depths is as complex and dangerous as exploring space. Like space travel, it requires very special equipment. You need a reliable source of oxygen. You also need protection from the cold and from the tremendous pressure of the water above you. The pressure could crush your lungs.

In scuba gear, you could safely dive to 91 m (300 ft.). To go below that, you would need to wear a rigid JIM suit (the first man to test it was named Jim). Even then, you could descend only to 457 m (1,500 ft.). To go still deeper, you would have to ride down in an undersea vehicle with a pressure-proof cabin, such as a submarine, a manned submersible, or a bathyscaphe.

In the submersible *Alvin,* for example, you could explore the ocean at a depth of about 4 km (2.5 mi.). And the bathyscaph *Trieste* could take you to the deepest part of the ocean—the Mariana Trench *(page 75)*.

Unmanned submersibles, such as *Jason Jr.,* do not carry people. Their television cameras and robotic arms are operated by remote control. They can gather pictures and objects at depths unsafe for divers.

Nuclear Submarine
700 m (2,300 ft.)

Submersible Robot
1,200 m (4,000 ft.)

Alvin with Jason Jr.
4,000 m (13,000 ft.)

Trieste
11,035 m (36,205 ft.)

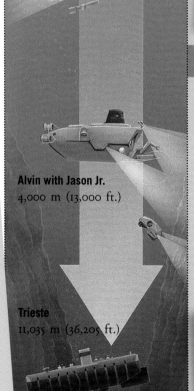

Jacques Yves Cousteau

Perhaps the most famous ocean scientist, or oceanographer, was France's Jacques Yves Cousteau *(below)*. In 1943, he and a friend, Émile Gagnan, invented the Self-Contained Underwater Breathing Apparatus, better known as SCUBA equipment.

Sylvia Earle

In 1979, American oceanographer Sylvia Earle earned the nickname of "Her Royal Deepness." She broke a record for the deepest underwater dive unconnected to the surface when she went down in a JIM suit to a depth of 381 m (1,250 ft.). Her dive was almost as deep as New York City's Empire State Building is high.

Now That's Pressure!

These two cups were the same size before they went on a 3,658-m (12,000-ft.) dive in the manned submersible *Alvin.* The cup on the right was with *Alvin*'s crew members in the pressure-proof cabin. The other cup was in an unprotected area of the sub. It was squeezed by the ocean's tremendous pressure—equal to the weight of five battleships—to half its normal size.

Diving in Style

To explore deep areas of the ocean, a diver must be encased in a special robotlike JIM suit. It protects the diver from the heavy water pressure in the deep ocean.

Fear of the Deep

In earlier times, people believed that the oceans were full of frightening monsters. Mapmakers warned sailors by drawing strange beasts in unexplored regions of the seas. Fierce-looking fishes and sea serpents (*right, top*) filled the ocean in a map of Iceland (*right*) drawn by Flemish geographer Abraham Ortelius in 1585.

The Challenger

Oceanography began in 1872, when the British ship *Challenger* (*right*) set out to explore the world's oceans. For four years, scientists gathered samples of seawaters and seabeds and studied them in cramped shipboard laboratories (*below*). They found 4,417 previously unknown species of undersea plants and animals.

Finding the *Titanic!*

The *Titanic* was 270 m (882 ft.) long. It had nine decks and was as tall as an 11-story building.

I n April 1912, the British luxury liner *Titanic* started its first voyage, a trip across the Atlantic Ocean. It was the biggest ship in the world. Its hull was steel, and its builders called it unsinkable.

But shortly before midnight on April 14, 1912, the great ship struck an iceberg. Water poured in through holes in the hull and, within hours, the *Titanic* sank. More than 1,500 of its 2,227 passengers and crew members died.

The *Titanic* broke in two as it plunged 4 km (2.5 mi.) to the ocean floor, where it lay for 73 years. Many people tried to find the ship, but the deep, treacherous waters and the total darkness defeated them. Then on September 1, 1985, a team of American and French oceanographers using underwater cameras saw the hulk.

The next year, the team's American leader, Robert Ballard, returned to explore the wreckage. In the submersible *Alvin,* he and two other scientists made the two-and-a-half-hour descent to the ocean floor. With the help of the robot *Jason Jr.,* they were able to take a series of incredible photographs of what was left of the great ship.

Icy Depths

In this very real-looking painting, *Alvin* explores the bow (front end) of the sunken *Titanic*. This is the ship's bridge, where the *Titanic's* captain, Edward J. Smith, had his headquarters for guiding the ship across the Atlantic. The pole lying across the bow is the ship's fallen foremast.

How Deep?

The *Titanic* sank to a depth of 3,965 m (12,460 ft.). This is more than 3.6 km (2.2 mi.) deeper than a scuba diver has ever gone and 3 km (1.9 mi.) deeper than naval submarines are able to dive.

Here's another way of thinking about how deep the *Titanic* sank: The Eiffel Tower in Paris, France, is 300 m (984 ft.) tall. Thirteen Eiffel Towers on top of each other would just about fill the distance between the *Titanic*'s wreckage and the ocean's surface.

The robot *Jason Jr.*, photographed from the submersible *Alvin*, peers into one of *Titanic*'s windows. *Alvin*'s crew members control *Jason Jr.* with a joystick. They nicknamed the robot the "swimming eyeball" because it lets them see into the hidden areas of the wreckage.

Empire State Building, New York
381 m (1,250 ft.)

Eiffel Tower, Paris
300 m (984 ft.)

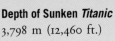

Depth of Sunken *Titanic*
3,798 m (12,460 ft.)

Grand Staircase

One of the most elegant features of the *Titanic*'s interior was the Grand Staircase (*above*). It was reserved for use by the ship's wealthiest passengers. Through a glass dome above the staircase, natural light streamed in and illuminated the elaborate oak paneling and intricately carved balustrades. A painting (*top*) shows what the *Jason Jr.* found when it explored the staircase shaft during *Alvin*'s third dive to the *Titanic*'s watery grave.

What Is an Iceberg?

An **iceberg** is a large, floating chunk of ice that has broken away from a glacier. The largest iceberg ever measured was a whopping 322 km (200 mi.) long and 97 km (60 mi.) wide. That's bigger than the entire country of Belgium. It was found floating near the South Pole. Icebergs in the Antarctic are usually bigger and flatter than those found in the Arctic Ocean, near the North Pole. This is because Antarctic icebergs break off from the huge, flat, floating shelves of glacial ice that surround the continent of Antarctica.

Usually about 90 percent of an iceberg is hidden underwater. That's why an iceberg is so dangerous to ships. Arctic icebergs are particularly dangerous because they drift toward the Atlantic Ocean, which has the world's busiest shipping lanes. Fortunately, icebergs melt as they float. By the time an Arctic iceberg reaches the Atlantic, it is usually only about a tenth of its original size.

An Iceberg Is Born

This photograph shows the formation of an iceberg off the coast of Alaska. A large piece of glacier breaks off and crashes into the frigid water. Once free of its parent glacier, the icy chunk will float out to sea as a new iceberg.

Looming Underneath

A ship sails dangerously close to the jagged peak of an iceberg. More perilous still is the part of the iceberg hidden under the water. You've heard the expression, "It's just the tip of the iceberg." This iceberg's tip—the peak poking up out of the water—is just one-tenth of the entire iceberg. Fortunately, ships that sail in icy waters have special equipment to warn them if they are too close to the hidden part of an iceberg.

Would You Believe?

Lassoing an Iceberg

What do you do when an iceberg 80 km (50 mi.) off the coast of Labrador is drifting on a collision course toward an oil-drilling ship? You lasso it and move it! A steel cable is looped around the iceberg. One end of the cable is attached to one ship and the other end is hooked to another ship. The ships then pull it out of the way.

For thousands of years, people have turned to the ocean for food, minerals, and energy. Fish and shellfish are an important part of the diets of people in many countries. Fish is also used to make such things as fertilizers and feed for farm animals. In fact, one-third of the 100 million metric tons of fish caught each year are used for something other than feeding people.

To extract salt from the ocean, flat areas on the shore are flooded with seawater. When the water evaporates, piles of salt are left behind to be harvested. Some hot, dry areas of the world also turn to the ocean for drinking water. Desalinization plants, built on the ocean's edge, remove salt from seawater, turning it into fresh water.

The most desirable resources in the ocean are **oil** and natural gas. Huge offshore oil and gas rigs pipe these resources up from beneath the ocean's floor. Some countries with strong tides have also figured out ways of using the ocean water to produce electricity by building tidal power stations.

This oil-drilling rig sits in the Gulf of Mexico off the Texas coast. Workers live on the rig, which can only be reached by boat or helicopter. A helipad provides a surface for landing helicopters.

Rising and falling tides can push enough water through a tunnel to run a fanlike turbine engine.

When seawater is allowed to evaporate, piles of salt are left behind for harvesting.

Sand and gravel are sucked up from the ocean floor to be used for making concrete and building highways

Strange But TRUE!

Manganese

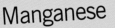

Strange, black, potato-sized lumps called **manganese nodules** litter the ocean's floor *(right)*. They contain up to 34 percent manganese, a metal used to make steel. They also contain iron, copper, cobalt, and nickel. They form when minerals in ocean water are deposited on the surface of a tiny object such as a piece of bone. It takes about a million years for a nodule to grow by one centimeter (.4 in.).

A desalinization plant on the coast of the Caribbean island of Curaçao removes salt from seawater, turning it into fresh water for drinking and agriculture.

Would **YOU** *Believe?*

Seaweed's Many Uses

Did you know that when you eat ice cream or brush your teeth, you are putting seaweed into your mouth? Substances extracted from a large brown seaweed called kelp are used to make many things you use every day, including tires, glass, paint, and soap. One of these substances, called algin, is put into ice cream and toothpaste to keep them smooth and creamy.

A desalinization plant removes salt from seawater so people can drink it.

To catch a lot of fish, boats surround schools of fish with huge nets and then drag them, and the fish, to the surface.

An ocean rig drills for oil trapped in rocks beneath the ocean floor.

Mineral-rich manganese nodules can be raked on the ocean floor and then sucked up to boats on the surface.

A ship cuts and harvests kelp, a giant, fast-growing seaweed that can quickly reach lengths of 60 m (200 ft.).

What Is the Atmosphere?

Look up at the **atmosphere**—that swirling mass of air hundreds of kilometers high. The Sun's heat keeps it in motion. If the Sun went away, the air would fall into a frigid snowdrift 6 m (20 ft.) deep. The atmosphere is all that stands between us and outer space.

Fortunately, sunlight keeps the atmosphere floating around Earth like a many-layered shield. The atmosphere protects us from the Sun's harmful rays and keeps Earth from getting too hot or too cold. It also has a useful mixture of gases that we can breathe. The most common one is nitrogen, followed by oxygen. The air also holds small but important amounts of water vapor and carbon dioxide, plus tiny dust particles.

Soaring over 700 km (430 mi.) into the sky, the atmosphere consists of five layers: from bottom to top they are the troposphere, stratosphere, mesosphere, thermosphere, and exosphere. The thick, cloud-filled troposphere is where weather happens. Beyond the first few kilometers, the air thins out rapidly as the molecules of air get farther apart. Finally, there is so little gravity that the last few air molecules easily escape into space.

The Layers of Earth's Atmosphere

The five main layers of the atmosphere are divided according to their temperatures. The lowest layer, the troposphere, varies in height around Earth depending on the warmth of its air. It is about 16 km (10 mi.) high at the warm equator, but only 9 km (6 mi.) high at the chilly poles.

Exosphere
480 km (300 mi.) and beyond

Thermosphere
80 to 480 km (50 to 300 mi.)

Mesosphere
50 to 80 km (30 to 50 mi.)

Stratosphere
10-16 to 50 km (6-10 to 30 mi.)

Troposphere
0 to 10-16 km (0 to 6-10 mi.)

The exosphere, where Earth's atmosphere fades into space, contains hardly any air, but its temperature can reach up to 1,650°C (3,000°F). Because the air is so thin, a person or spacecraft would not feel the heat.

The thermosphere's air is very thin, but it is thick enough to absorb the Sun's ultraviolet light. This light, which is invisible to human eyes, heats the thermosphere up to 1,480°C (2,700°F).

The mesosphere, the coldest layer, doesn't absorb much of the Sun's heat or ultraviolet light, so its temperature can drop to -90°C (-130°F). The air is thick enough to slow down and burn up meteorites.

The stratosphere has most of the ozone layer, which absorbs almost all of the Sun's harmful ultraviolet light. Because of this, the air warms up to 4°C (40°F).

The troposphere is the thick, heavy, moist layer closest to Earth's surface. Warmest at ground level, it cools with altitude to as low as -70°C (-58°F).

Let's Compare

Planetary Atmospheres

At 150 million km (93 million mi.) from the Sun, Earth is in just the right spot to support life. It is the only planet known to have enough liquid water and plenty of oxygen to breathe. Venus, closer to the Sun, is a roiling inferno of poisonous gas clouds. Mars, farther away, has a thin, freezing atmosphere.

Earth

Venus

Mars

Seen from the space shuttle *Discovery,* the Moon rises over Earth's atmosphere, which clings to the planet like a thin blue shell. Clouds cover more than half of Earth's surface.

Fast FACTS

Where will you find Earth's wildest weather?

Coldest Polyus Nedostupnosti (Pole of Inaccessibility), Antarctica: average temperature -58.2°C (-72°F)

Hottest Dallol, Ethiopia: annual average temperature 34.4°C (94°F)

Wettest Mawsynram, Meghalaya State, India: average annual rainfall 1,187 cm (467.5 in.)

Driest Atacama Desert, Chile: average annual rainfall less than .08mm (.003 in.)

Windiest Commonwealth Bay, George V Coast, Antarctica: gales up to 320 km/h (200 mph)

Least Sunshine South Pole: no sunshine for 182 days of the year; North Pole: no sunshine for 176 days

Craziest Jump in Temperature Spearfish, South Dakota, USA, on January 22, 1943: in 2 minutes from -20°C (-4°F) to 7°C (45°F)

Highest Recorded (Shade) Temperature Al-'Aziziya, Iraq on September. 13, 1922: 57.8°C (136°F)

Lowest Temperature Recorded Vostok, Antarctica, July 21, 1983: 89.5°C (-128.6°F)

Why Does the Sky Change Color?

If air is invisible—which it is, pretty much—why can't we see straight into outer space? Why is the daytime sky blue? Why does it change to red at sunset, and then, seemingly, vanish at night to show us the stars? The answers to these questions all lie in the way that sunlight mixes with air.

Sunlight looks invisible to us, but in fact it is made of all the colors in the rainbow. When the colors of light mix together, the light is called white light.

As sunlight travels through space, it moves in waves like the surface of the ocean. Each color of light has its own **wavelength**—the distance between the top of one wave and the top of the next. Blue and violet light have the shortest wavelengths, so they would look like lots of little choppy waves. Red and orange have the longest wavelengths; they would look like long rolling waves.

When this sea of light hits our **atmosphere,** it crashes into zillions of tiny obstacles—air molecules, water droplets, ice crystals, and dust particles. The light starts to bounce around as it hits these objects, in a process known as **scattering.** Blue light, with its short waves, gets scattered the most, and so its blue color shows up in the sky on a clear, sunny day.

At sunrise or sunset, sunlight follows a longer path through more air in the atmosphere. This allows the sunlight to meet up with more dust and water vapor. The shorter, bluish wavelengths of light scatter so completely that we see only the longer wavelengths of red, orange, and yellow. They are less affected by the tiny obstacles they meet, so they pass on through to our eyes, revealing themselves as the colors of the twilight.

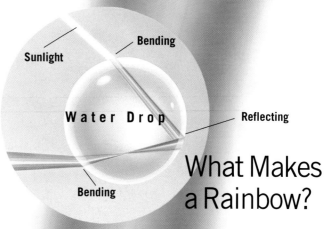

People Sir Isaac Newton

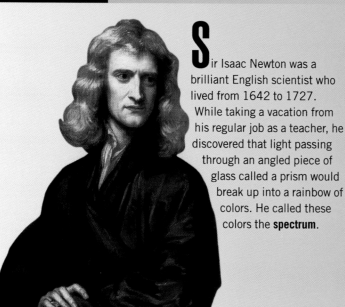

Sir Isaac Newton was a brilliant English scientist who lived from 1642 to 1727. While taking a vacation from his regular job as a teacher, he discovered that light passing through an angled piece of glass called a prism would break up into a rainbow of colors. He called these colors the **spectrum**.

What Makes a Rainbow?

When sunlight shines into a drop of water, the water acts like a prism. When light enters the drop it is bent and splits into the colors of the spectrum: red, orange, yellow, green, blue, indigo, and violet. The light then reflects, or bounces, off the back of the water drop and bends again as it leaves the drop, so that the colors fan out widely into a bright, glorious rainbow.

Blue Skies and Red Skies

When the Sun is high in the sky, sunlight has less distance to travel through the atmosphere. The air scatters the short wavelengths of blue light so that we see them coloring the sky.

When the Sun is low in the sky, sunlight travels through more of the atmosphere. Blue light is scattered away completely. Only the longer wavelengths of red, orange, and yellow light make it all the way to our eyes.

The sky is constantly changing colors, mostly because of dust and other particles floating in the air. On a clear day the sky appears bright blue because the particles in the air are very tiny and they scatter blue light the best. When volcanoes spew ash into the air, sunsets become fiery red, because these large particles do a great job scattering red light.

Sun High in Sky

Sun Low in Sky

Strange But TRUE!

The Brocken Specter

Up in the mountains, when conditions are right, you can cast your shadow on a cloud. Sometimes called a Brocken specter (named after a mountain peak in Germany), the phenomenon occurs only when the Sun is low in the sky and directly behind you. The sunlight casts your enlarged shadow ahead onto misty fog or cloud droplets. Often the shadow is surrounded by a rainbow-like halo.

The Water Cycle

Earth is an ocean planet: almost three-quarters of its surface is covered in water. But if that water stayed peacefully in the oceans, all life on Earth would die of thirst. Fortunately, the planet has something called the **water cycle.** Driven by heat from the Sun, enormous amounts of water move between the oceans and land. This never-ending exchange gives us the water we drink every day.

Let's start with the oceans, which hold almost all the water on Earth. Warmed by the Sun, every year about one-quarter of the oceans' water **evaporates,** or changes from a **liquid** to a vapor. This moist air quickly rises into the atmosphere. Carried by winds, often for great distances, the water **vapor** starts to cool. When it has cooled enough, it **condenses,** turning into tiny droplets of water that clump together to form clouds. From these clouds, the water then returns to Earth in the form of rain or snow.

Most of this water drops right back into the ocean, completing the cycle. The rest of the moisture drifts over land, mingling with vapor rising from rivers, lakes, soil, and plants. Eventually that water, too, falls to the ground as rain or snow. Some of it soaks into the soil or seeps deeper underground. Some freezes into icecaps and **glaciers.** On the surface, rainwater runs off into rivers and lakes. The force of gravity slowly pulls the water to the oceans to start the cycle again.

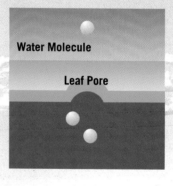

Transpiration

Water can evaporate from plants as well as from oceans and rivers. Most of a plant's water escapes through tiny open pores on a leaf's surface. This kind of evaporation is called **transpiration.**

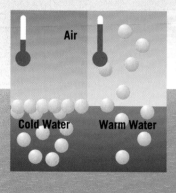

Evaporation

Evaporation begins with heat. Heat from the Sun makes water molecules start to move around. Eventually, they bump around so much that they break free of the bonds that hold them together and float off as water vapor. The higher the temperature, the more molecules will escape.

Three States of Water

Water is amazing. It is the only thing on Earth that can exist at the same time in all three forms: solid, liquid, and gas. Water's form depends on how tightly its molecules stick together. The molecules of solid water, or ice, are locked together so they can't move. The molecules of liquid water move about freely, letting water take the shape of its container. Molecules of gaseous water, or vapor, do not stick together at all, so they escape into the air.

Water Vapor

Water

Ice

Snow

When water vapor in clouds gets cold enough, it freezes into tiny crystals. These crystals grow into the six-sided snowflakes that drift down to Earth's surface.

Snow Crystals

Rain

As the water vapor in clouds condenses, it turns into larger and larger droplets. After a while, the droplets start to fall. As they fall, they bump into each other, forming bigger drops. These big drops become the rain that falls to the ground.

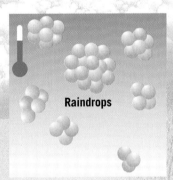

Raindrops

Glacier

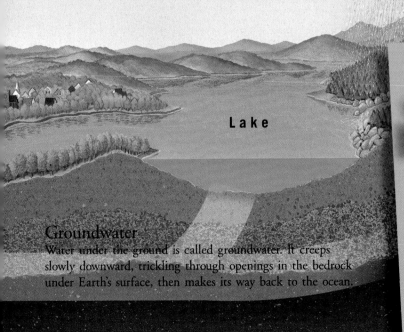

Lake

Groundwater

Water under the ground is called groundwater. It creeps slowly downward, trickling through openings in the bedrock under Earth's surface, then makes its way back to the ocean.

Would You Believe?

These beakers show where to find all the water on Earth. Almost all of it is in the oceans, with just a little in the ground, ice, rivers, lakes, and air. Earth got its water billions of years ago when it was a very young planet. Since then the same water has been used and reused.

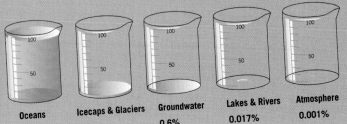

| Oceans 97.2% | Icecaps & Glaciers 2% | Groundwater 0.6% | Lakes & Rivers 0.017% | Atmosphere 0.001% |

What Are Clouds?

You can make your own cloud: Just breathe out on a cold day. When the damp, warm air from your lungs meets the cold air outside, the water **vapor** in your breath **condenses.** That means the vapor turns into little drops of water. These droplets are big enough to be seen but still light enough to float. That's a cloud.

Clouds in the sky are made of billions of tiny water droplets or ice **crystals.** They have three basic forms, depending on how high up they are. Thin, wispy, high-level **cirrus** clouds are made of ice crystals. Middle-level altostratus and altocumulus clouds are sheets or puffy patterned clouds made of water droplets that let the Sun shine through. Low-lying, flat sheets of water droplets are called **stratus** clouds. All other clouds are a variation or combination of these three types. If you study them closely, they can help you predict the weather.

How Clouds Are Formed

When the Sun heats the ground, the air above the ground warms and starts to rise. The warmest air pockets rise the fastest, carrying moisture from the ground. As the moist air rises, it cools, until it reaches the temperature known as the condensation level, where water vapor turns into water droplets. Billions of droplets combine into a cloud that drifts off, with others forming in its place.

Cold Air

Condensation Level

Warm Air

Warm Ground

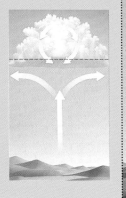

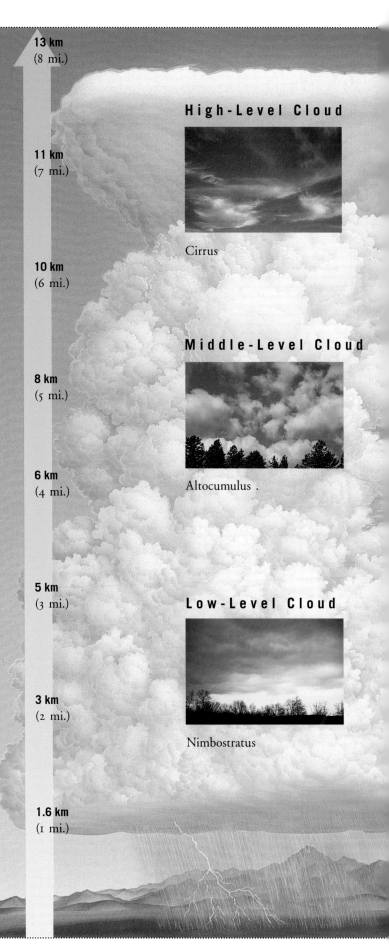

13 km (8 mi.)

11 km (7 mi.)

10 km (6 mi.)

8 km (5 mi.)

6 km (4 mi.)

5 km (3 mi.)

3 km (2 mi.)

1.6 km (1 mi.)

High-Level Cloud

Cirrus

Middle-Level Cloud

Altocumulus .

Low-Level Cloud

Nimbostratus

The 10 Types of Clouds

Cirrocumulus
Thin, patchy, fluffy waves or ripples; rain likely later

Cirrus
Thin, milky-white, wispy strands; fair weather

Cirrostratus
Very thin sheets; may mean a change in weather

Altocumulus
Patchy rolls of puffy white to gray clouds; precipitation later

Altostratus
Smooth sheets of gray cloud; possible light rain or snow

Stratocumulus
Soft, low sheets of gray or white rounded clouds joined together; possible light rain or snow

Cumulonimbus
Towering, dark clouds, sometimes spreading out to form an anvil top; heavy rain, lightning, and thunder; possible hail or tornadoes

Cumulus
Dense, puffy white clouds that pile up from a flat base; fair weather

Stratus
Low sheets forming even layer across the sky; unsettled weather

Nimbostratus
Low, thick layer of dark clouds covering the sky; steady rain or snow

People | Luke Howard

The Cloud Namer

In 1803, Luke Howard, an English weather watcher, came up with the simple system of naming clouds that is still used today. His Latin names described three basic cloud shapes: "cumulus," or heap; "stratus," or layer; and "cirrus," or curl. Sometimes he put these names together or added "nimbus" for rain or "alto" for height to describe cloud combinations.

Strange But TRUE!

Looking like a fleet of alien spacecraft, huge flying-saucer-shaped clouds hover over Santos, Brazil. These lenticular, or lens-shaped, clouds formed on waves of air downwind from the mountain peaks seen in the distance. As they rose to the crest of the waves and cooled, the clouds formed their distinctive lens shape. Sometimes lenticular clouds like these are mistaken for unidentified flying objects (UFOs).

Rain Snow and Hail

Cats and dogs do not really rain from the sky, despite what people say. However, huge flakes of snow, torrents of rain, misty drizzle, and pounding hailstones do fall from the clouds all the time. These varied forms of water are called **precipitation.**

Most precipitation starts off as snow or rain in the frigid air of a cloud. Snowflakes form when very cold water freezes onto an ice **crystal** falling slowly through a cloud. The temperature and the amount of moisture in the cloud decide the shape of the flake. If the air is very cold, the snowflakes look like tiny, six-sided columns. Large, branching, star-shaped snowflakes form when the air is warmer.

If the snow drops into warmer air below the cloud, it melts and hits the ground as rain. Only in the tropics does rain start as rain inside clouds. Inside the clouds, tiny water droplets bump into each other to form bigger drops. These bigger drops start to fall, collecting more droplets along the way. Eventually, the drops are big enough to fall to the ground as rain without drying up on the way down.

Let's Compare

Cloud Droplets to Raindrops

Mist Droplet

Cloud Droplet

Drizzle Droplet

It takes about a million cloud droplets to form an average raindrop. Cloud droplets are small enough to float. The heavier mist, drizzle, and raindrops fall to the ground.

Raindrop

What Falling Raindrops Look Like

Small raindrops stay round, never teardrop-shaped, as they are falling.

Larger drops start to look like hamburger buns: flattened on the bottom with the sides bulging out.

The raindrop can only reach about 0.6 cm (.25 in.) across before it divides into even smaller drops.

On a roller-coaster ride through a storm cloud, tiny pellets of ice collide with very cold water droplets. As the droplets freeze around the ice pellets, they add thin skinlike layers of ice. Finally these hailstones become so heavy that they fall to Earth.

In 1970, the heaviest hailstone measured in the United States landed in a yard in Coffeyville, Kansas. The big chunk of ice weighed 0.75 kg (1.6 lbs.) and was 14 cm (5.5 in.) wide *(above)*.

How Is Hail Formed?

How Big?

How long does it take eight people to make a 27-meter-high (90-foot) snowman? Just 21 days! Built in the mountains of Switzerland in 1993, this immense snow sculpture was constructed out of solid snow and water. The sculptors towed the snow to the site and then created the rest by hand, using ladders to reach the higher parts. Huge pieces of felt were used to make up his face, hat, buttons, and scarf.

People — Wilson A. Bentley

Wilson A. Bentley was very fascinated by snowflakes from the age of 15. In 1885, he hooked up a special camera to a microscope and took the first successful photographs of snowflakes. For the next 40 years, standing outside in the cold with his bulky camera, he photographed and cataloged thousands of snowflakes. Every one had six sides, but no two were exactly alike. His lifelong study earned him the nickname "Snowflake" Bentley.

Fast FACTS

 One inch of rain falling over an acre of ground equals 102,747 l (27,143 gal.) of water

 Most rain in 24 hours: 1,870 mm (73.62 in.), island of Réunion, Indian Ocean, March 15-16, 1952

 Heaviest rainburst: 38.1 mm (1.5 in.), in 1.5 minutes, island of Guadeloupe, West Indies, 1970

 Most snow in 24 hours: 198 cm (78 in.), Mile 47 Camp, Cooper River Division 4, Alaska, February 7, 1963

 Most snow in single snowstorm: 480 cm (189 inches), Mount Shasta, California, USA, February 13-19, 1959

What Are Floods?

On July 31, 1976, people in the Big Thompson Canyon of Colorado tried to stay dry as some 30 cm (12 in.) of rain poured down in just four hours. Then, trapped between high rock walls, the Big Thompson River roared through the canyon in a flash flood. It killed at least 135 people, making it one of the worst flash floods in U.S. history.

A flood happens when water rises and overflows onto normally dry land. There are several kinds of floods. Flash floods occur with little warning when heavy rain falls on soil that cannot absorb or drain all the extra water. They tend to be confined to one area. Broadscale floods are slower, but farther-reaching. These might happen when heavy snowmelt soaks the ground, causing rivers and lakes to overflow day after day. Some of the most destructive floods are caused by tropical storms. These storms form over oceans and can drop trillions of liters of rain in 24 hours.

Hero Dog

Would You Believe?

When water flooded their warehouse, the Goodriches of California got busy bailing. Then they remembered their dog Tasha and her newborn pups, shut in a back room. When they ran to the rescue, they found Tasha treading water and steadying her bobbing dog dish, into which she had placed the seven pups.

Mighty Mississippi on the Move

In the summer of 1993, unusual weather attacked the midwestern United States. Record amounts of rain fell, flooding towns and farms. Floodwaters swept away this house, but the people in it made it safely to high ground.

Rivers and lakes

usually overflow their banks slowly and steadily, giving people plenty of time to escape—but floodwaters can linger. Residents, like this boy in a midwestern U.S. town, must learn new ways of getting around. Hundreds of hours of cleanup lie ahead.

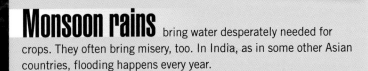

Monsoon rains

bring water desperately needed for crops. They often bring misery, too. In India, as in some other Asian countries, flooding happens every year.

Tropical storms

can hurl raging floods over coastal lands. Rescue workers in Puerto Rico saved this baby and four family members, but others were not so lucky.

Energy from the Sun

On a sunny day, it's easy to believe the Sun is responsible for Earth's weather. But the Sun is equally responsible for stormy weather. In fact, energy from the Sun is at the root of all weather in our **atmosphere.**

The secret lies in how the Sun heats the curved surface of Earth. It is hotter at the equator, where the Sun beams down directly overhead. It is cooler at the poles, where the Sun lies lower in the sky and strikes Earth at an angle. This angle causes the energy to spread out over a wider area. (With a flashlight in a darkened room, you can illustrate the effect yourself. Shine the light straight down at your feet. Then slant it to the floor across the room. Does the pool of light change size? Each pool of light has the same amount of energy, but in the smaller pool, energy is concentrated, as it is in sunlight at the equator.)

Uneven heating changes the balance of the Sun's energy in Earth's atmosphere. Warm air at the equator rises and moves toward the polar regions. Cool air there sinks and moves toward the equator. The constantly moving air creates wind and weather.

Sun's Energy Turns to Heat Energy

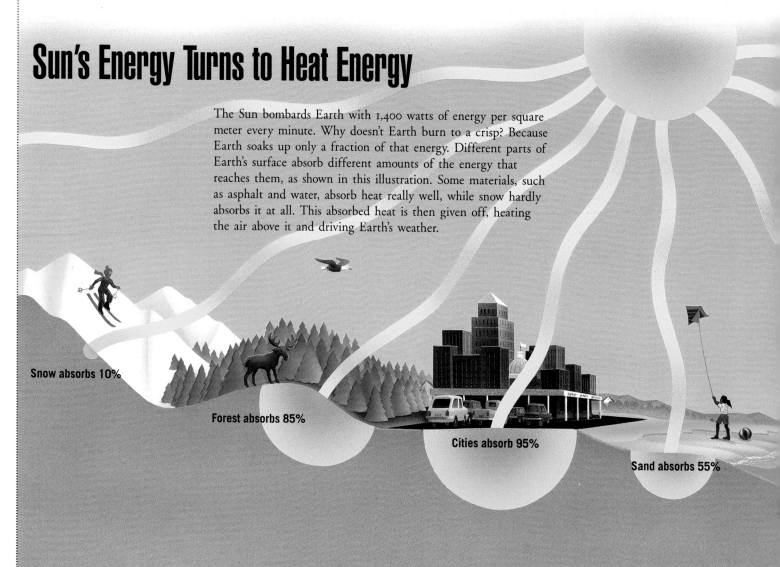

The Sun bombards Earth with 1,400 watts of energy per square meter every minute. Why doesn't Earth burn to a crisp? Because Earth soaks up only a fraction of that energy. Different parts of Earth's surface absorb different amounts of the energy that reaches them, as shown in this illustration. Some materials, such as asphalt and water, absorb heat really well, while snow hardly absorbs it at all. This absorbed heat is then given off, heating the air above it and driving Earth's weather.

Snow absorbs 10%

Forest absorbs 85%

Cities absorb 95%

Sand absorbs 55%

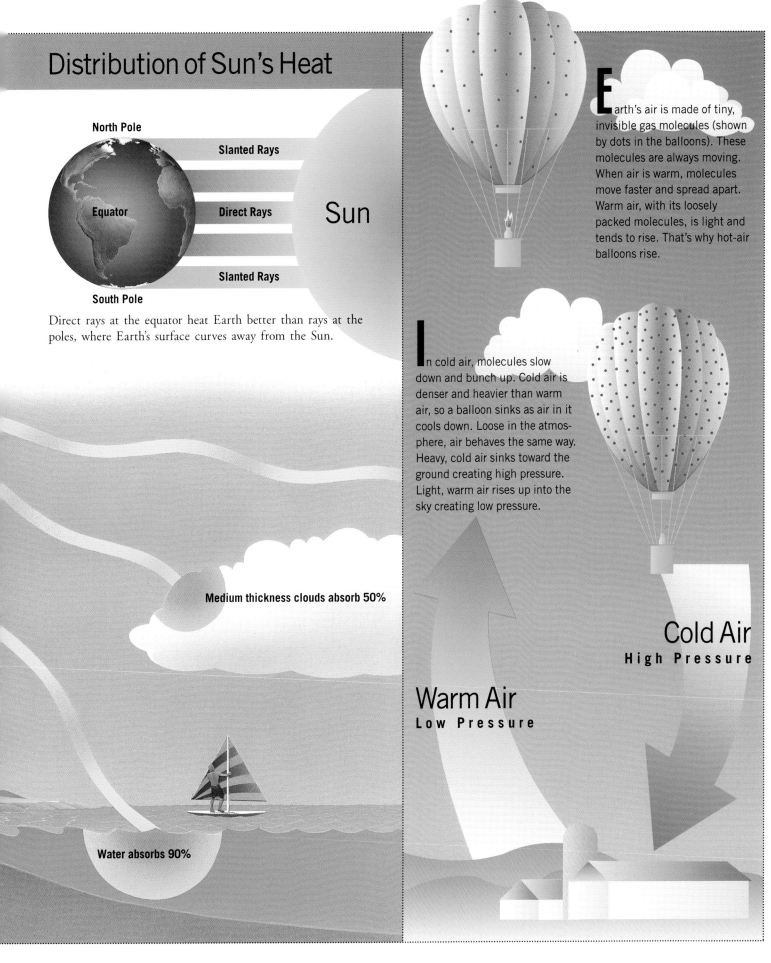

Distribution of Sun's Heat

North Pole

Slanted Rays

Equator

Direct Rays

Sun

Slanted Rays

South Pole

Direct rays at the equator heat Earth better than rays at the poles, where Earth's surface curves away from the Sun.

Earth's air is made of tiny, invisible gas molecules (shown by dots in the balloons). These molecules are always moving. When air is warm, molecules move faster and spread apart. Warm air, with its loosely packed molecules, is light and tends to rise. That's why hot-air balloons rise.

In cold air, molecules slow down and bunch up. Cold air is denser and heavier than warm air, so a balloon sinks as air in it cools down. Loose in the atmosphere, air behaves the same way. Heavy, cold air sinks toward the ground creating high pressure. Light, warm air rises up into the sky creating low pressure.

Medium thickness clouds absorb 50%

Cold Air
H i g h   P r e s s u r e

Warm Air
L o w   P r e s s u r e

Water absorbs 90%

Where Does Wind Come From?

I n the days when ships relied on **wind,** sailors dreaded crossing the equator. Along it lies a belt of nearly windless low pressure called the doldrums. Here ships could lie motionless for weeks, running short of water and food. Once through the doldrums, sailors knew they would find a broad band of global winds called the trade winds, and after those, the westerlies.

The reason sailors knew where they might meet certain winds is that the Sun heats Earth in the same way all the time. The resulting air movement creates bands of predictable winds around the globe. These are called **prevailing winds.**

Wind is made by differences in **air pressure.** Warm air, heated by the surface below, rises. Cool air from colder places rushes in to replace it, creating wind.

The land also affects wind. Forests slow wind down by blocking its way, and the height and location of buildings can influence the speed and direction of wind. Coastal areas almost always have a breeze. That's why they're a good place for hang gliders, such as the one at right—and their dogs!

Aeolus (*above*), a god from the Greek myths, was guardian of the wind, which he kept in a sack swirling around him. He let storms out at his own whim and at the gods' commands. Aeolus is one of a many wind gods that early cultures used to explain fickle winds. Ancient Aztecs believed their monkey-like wind god Ehecatl blew the Sun across the sky every day.

Land and Sea Breezes

Sea breezes form along the shore because land heats up and cools down faster than water. On a sunny day, air over land quickly warms and rises, creating a zone of low pressure. Cool, high-pressure ocean air pours into the low-pressure area fast enough to make a breeze. At night, the situation changes. Land cools quickly. Air over it now has higher pressure than sea air, and so the cycle reverses.

Daytime Sea Breeze

Nighttime Land Breeze

Global Winds

Cold at Poles

Warm

Hot at Equator

Warm

Cold at Poles

Polar Easterlies

Westerlies

NE Trades

SE Trades

Westerlies

Polar Easterlies

The globe at top shows "cells" of air movement caused by Earth's unequal heating. As warm air rises, cold air rushes across to take its place. High above, warm air cools and sinks. These huge circulating heat exchanges create global winds that are more or less a permanent feature of Earth. The lower globe shows their directions and names. Earth's rotation spins the winds out to either side, causing them to blow at an angle.

What Is Weather?

What you feel when you step outside—wind, rain, snow, or sunshine—is **weather.** Weather has six main parts: temperature, atmospheric pressure, wind, **humidity, precipitation,** and cloudiness.

We have weather because the Sun heats Earth unevenly. Sunlight warms places near the equator more than places near the poles. It heats land more than oceans. As this happens, great rafts of air, heated to the temperature of Earth's surface, arise over these areas and move away. These **air masses** chase each other around the planet, clashing and mixing. They cause most of the weather below.

Air masses may stretch over thousands of kilometers. As long as one mass lies overhead, weather is relatively settled, whether fair or foul. Then a shift in the wind can blow one air mass away and push in a new one. The edges where two air masses meet are called **fronts.** This is where stormy, changeable weather occurs, as if two vast armies were battling overhead.

Weatherman Wannabes

Groundhog

Pine Cones

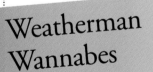

Closed   Open

If a groundhog sees its shadow on February 2, there will be six more weeks of winter. At least, so says American folklore. A pine cone makes a better forecaster. In dry weather, its scales open up and curl out. When rain is on the way, the scales sponge up dampness in the air and the cone swells shut.

Weather Symbols

Fronts

 Cold Front
Warm Front
Stationary Front

Pressure Symbols

High   Low

Wind Speeds

Light Wind
High Wind
Hurricane Force

Precipitation / Other

Drizzle
Rain
Snow
Hail
Freezing Rain
Fog
Haze

No Clouds
Partly Cloudy
Very Cloudy
Completely Overcast

Storms

Tornado
Thunderstorm
Lightning
Tropical Storm
Hurricane

Sunny Day

A mass of cold air moves over a city. Cold air can't hold much water **vapor,** so this air mass delivers fine weather, sunny and dry. At the leading edge of the cold air mass, called a cold front, it's a different story.

Weather Moves In

Cold Air Mass

Cold Front

Would You Believe?

In mere minutes, a fluffy cloud swells to a towering thunderhead twice as high as Mount Everest. Packing more power than an atomic bomb, the cloud will hammer the ground below with lightning, thunder, strong winds and rain. Such anvil-shaped clouds, called cumulonim-bus, occur where a cold air mass crashes into a warm air mass—a cold front. The clouds can take shape, unleash a storm, break up, and vanish all in the space of an hour.

Stormy Day

Here the cold front crashes into the edge of a warm air mass. The heavier cold air shoves the warm air steeply upward. In this zone of mixing air masses, thunderclouds build rapidly. Lightning, thunder, rain, and high winds shake the ground. High above, a fast-moving river of air called the jet stream pushes the storms along. They don't last long.

Rainy Day

Here a warm front overtakes a cold air mass. The lighter, warmer air slides up and over the cold air, creating a gently sloping edge. As the warm front slowly rises, it cools a little and can no longer hold as much water vapor. The vapor **condenses** into raindrops. That's why warm fronts promise days of steady rain.

Warm Air Mass

Cold Air Mass

Warm Front

Predicting the Weather

The greatest detective work on Earth goes into the everyday job of predicting the **weather.** All over the world—and from high above it—machines measure **wind** speed and direction, cloud types, **air pressure,** and more. The numbers flash to weather offices, where powerful computers put them together, helping scientists predict the weather.

From sailors heading out to sea to school kids heading off to the bus, millions of people depend on weather reports. Television, radio, and the Internet all play a vital role in getting weather information to people. Sometimes it's a matter of life and death. As one rescue director put it, a timely storm warning can mean "the difference between survival and 10,000 tombstones."

Just how accurate are weather reports? Short-range forecasts, predicting weather for the next 24 hours, can be 90 percent accurate. Long-range forecasts, predicting a week's weather, are much less reliable. That's because so many things, big and little, affect our weather.

What's a Meteorologist?

A meteorologist is a scientist who studies the weather. ("Meteor" comes from a Greek word that means "up in the air.") Meteorologists collect information from weather satellites and other machines. Then they use computers to study the information and, they hope, predict the weather. Some meteorologists appear on TV to tell the public what tomorrow's weather will be. Alan Sealls *(right)* is a TV meteorologist in Chicago.

Take a casual look at a weather report. You may not know that a radar station in Nevada, a buoy bobbing in the Atlantic, a ship off the South American coast, a weather balloon over Texas, a commercial airliner over the Pacific, and a satellite in space may all have had a say in it. This illustration shows some of the ways weather sleuths get the goods. Meteorologists will take the bare numbers that flow into the office and boil them down to an understandable message: Sunny today, let's play ball!

Weather Balloon

Automated Ground Station

Ground Station

Radar

Commercial Airline

Weather Ship

Keeping Watch Over Earth

Satellite

Weather Buoy

Hurricane Hunter

Weather Instruments

Barometer

A barometer measures atmospheric, or air, pressure. An aneroid barometer *(left)* contains metal that compresses when air pressure rises and expands when air pressure falls. The metal is connected to a dial that can then display the amount of pressure.

Anemometer

An anemometer *(right)* measures wind speed. As the wind blows, the anemometer's cups spin. The speed of the cups gets translated into wind speed. This number then appears on a meter or an electronic display.

Rain Gauge

A rain gauge *(left)* measures amount of **precipitation.** Its funnel-mouthed cylinder catches rain and shows the amount in centimeters or inches. Observers record the number and then empty it at specific times.

Thermometer

A thermometer measures air temperature. Mercury in the thermometer's vacuum tube expands as air warms it and shrinks as colder air cools it. To make sure readings are accurate, thermometers must be protected from direct sunlight and hot surfaces. They are often kept inside a shelter like the one at right, sometimes called a weather shack.

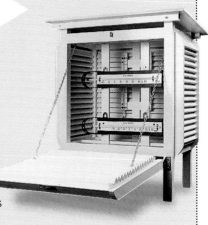

What Is Lightning?

If you've ever gotten a shock from a metal doorknob, you've felt firsthand the electrical forces that make lightning. Shuffling your feet on the carpet as you approached the door created friction. The friction built up negative electrical charges on your body. These charges made a spark jump from you to the positively charged metal doorknob. Ouch!

Friction in thunderclouds creates electric charges, too: negative ones. Under the storm, the ground becomes positively charged. Lightning occurs when the two charges become so intense they can surge across open air and meet.

Electricity doesn't travel easily through open air. That's why you don't get a shock until your hand is nearly touching the doorknob. And that's why lightning strikes whatever is closest to the clouds—a tree, a building, and sometimes even a person. In the United States, 400 people are struck by lightning in an average year. About 100 of those don't survive the encounter.

Fast FACTS

 In its tenth-of-a-second lifetime, a lightning bolt creates enough energy to light up all of New York City.

 Lightning can heat the air around it to 30,000°C (54,000°F), which is five times hotter than the surface of the Sun.

 During a thunderstorm, stay indoors and don't use electrical appliances such as phones and computers.

 If caught outside, stay away from trees. Squat down and tuck your head low, but don't lie on the ground. Lightning can run along the wet ground and zap you.

 Sound travels about 1.6 km (1 mi.) in five seconds. To find out how far away lightning is, count the seconds between "flash" and "bang" and divide by five.

When lightning strikes sandy soil, it can bore right down into it, fusing earth into sand-encrusted branches of glass. These "lightning scars" are called fulgurites, named for the Latin word for lightning. Fulgurites can measure 4.5 m (15 ft.) long.

Would **You** *Believe?*

Maryland teenager Toy Trice still doesn't like to talk about the brush with lightning that almost killed him. He was at football practice when it struck, bashing a hole in his helmet, torching his jersey, and blowing his shoes off. Toy stopped breathing but was revived on the spot. If first aid is applied quickly, as it was in Toy's case, your chances of surviving a lightning strike are surprisingly good.

Lightning and Thunder

Lightning threatens when water drops hit each other inside a thundercloud, building up a negative electric charge in the base of the cloud. This creates a positive charge on the ground below.

When negative charges swoop to within 50 m (164 ft.) of the ground or a tall object, electric current surges across the gap between them. In a fraction of a second, lightning flickers up and back several times.

Lightning scorches air around it. The hot air expands and vibrates. This quick twanging of the air creates the crackling, rumbling sounds we call thunder.

Boom!

What Are Hurricanes?

Hurricanes are spinning tropical storms with winds of at least 119 km (74 mi.) per hour. They are born over tropical seas just north or south of the equator, where the water is warm and the air is heavy with water vapor.

Hurricanes start off as bands of thunderstorms that begin spinning when they collide with trade winds. As the storm winds draw warm air upward, huge amounts of water vapor change to rain. This process gives off energy called **latent heat.** Latent heat is the fuel that whips ordinary storms into a monstrous spiral of wind and rain hundreds of kilometers wide.

An average hurricane drops more than 9 trillion liters (2.4 trillion gal.) of rain every day. Built up by the winds, a wall of seawater up to 7.5 m (25 ft.) high forms under the storm. When it hits land, this storm surge, rain, and wind can cause great damage. In 1991, a hurricane struck Bangladesh, killing 135,000 people. Mercifully, hurricanes can't last long once they are inland.

Where Do Hurricanes Occur?

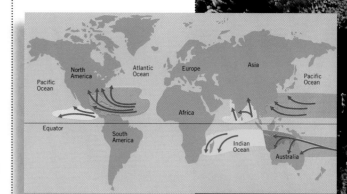

Hurricanes form in seven ocean basins around the world. They have different names in different countries. In the western Pacific they are known as typhoons, while in Australia and countries found around the Indian Ocean they are called tropical cyclones.

Anatomy of a Hurricane

In the center of a hurricane is the "eye"—an area of calm, clear air. Winds there flow downward.

A hurricane's cloud walls reach 15 km (9 mi.) high. Winds spiral in at the bottom, spin violently around, then zoom out at the top.

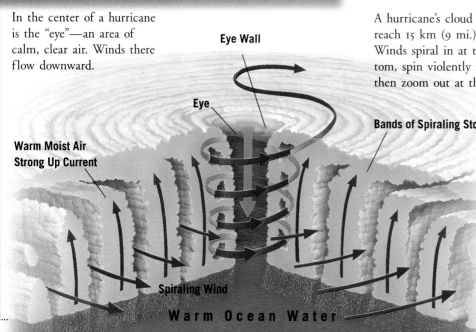

Eye Wall

Eye

Bands of Spiraling Storm Clouds

Warm Moist Air Strong Up Current

Spiraling Wind

Warm Ocean Water

A satellite photo shows Hurricane Fran—beautiful and deadly—hurtling toward the U.S. coast in 1996.

Hurricanes Close Up

"Spectacular," says hurricane hunter Jack Parrish of the view from inside the eye of the storm. "A ring of clouds towers above you, the water boils below."

I Was There!

I've flown into the eye of a hurricane 330 times now. Believe it or not, the very worst time up was my second day on the job. We got stuck in the eye wall, where winds were 180 miles per hour, for something like 12 or 13 minutes—it seemed like a lifetime. Usually we just punch right through. We were strapped in tight, but the plane was rocketing up and down like a wild roller-coaster ride. I think it's safe to say we all thought we'd probably die. When we finally got back to base, the entire inside of the plane was a shambles. One man quit on the spot. Usually we're in for a smoother ride. And it's still a lot more fun than working at a desk! We meteorologists just like to get out and look at the weather, I guess.

Astronauts on board the space shuttle took this picture looking down on the eye of a hurricane.

Jack Parrish and his crew use big transport planes to fly into storms.

Hurricane Force!

Like forgotten toys in an empty bathtub, Florida power-boats lie tumbled together where Hurricane Andrew dropped them in 1992 *(left)*. In the same year, more than half the houses on the Hawaiian island of Kauai were demolished *(center)* by Hurricane Iniki, the most powerful storm to hit the island in the 20th century. Three years earlier, Hurricane Hugo pummeled the U.S. Virgin Islands with 257 km/h (160 mph) winds *(below)*.

What Is a Tornado?

In 1946, gold coins rained down on a Russian town. A column of wind touched down from a thunderstorm, tore the treasure from its hiding place, and showered the town with money. The windy thief was a **tornado,** a violently spinning funnel of air.

Although tornadoes occur in many parts of the world, three-quarters of them happen in the United States. Most rip along a corridor known as Tornado Alley that stretches from Texas to Iowa. Here, warm, moist air from the Gulf of Mexico gets trapped under cold, dry air from Canada carried south by the **winds** of the jet stream. Strong winds blow over weaker ones, setting air spinning around a center of low pressure. The low pressure gives tornadoes their suction power.

Most tornadoes are classified on the Fujita scale. F0 and F1 tornadoes are "weak," with winds up to 180 km/h (112 mph). F2 and F3 are "strong," up to 331 km/h (206 mph). And a terrifying few, two of every hundred, are F4s and F5s—"violent." The largest may be more 1.6 km (1 mi.) wide, with winds around 495 km/h (308 mph).

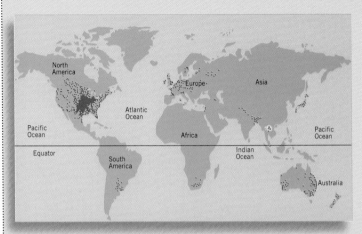

Dotted areas show that tornadoes strike all populated continents but occur most often in North America.

What's in a Tornado?

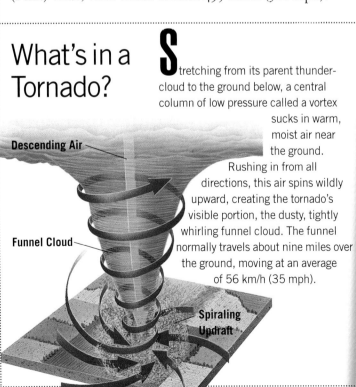

Stretching from its parent thundercloud to the ground below, a central column of low pressure called a vortex sucks in warm, moist air near the ground. Rushing in from all directions, this air spins wildly upward, creating the tornado's visible portion, the dusty, tightly whirling funnel cloud. The funnel normally travels about nine miles over the ground, moving at an average of 56 km/h (35 mph).

Descending Air

Funnel Cloud

Spiraling Updraft

Strange But TRUE!

Sailors from ancient times to the present have told of fish raining down on the decks. Modern meteorologists believe the fish dropped from waterspouts, eerie twisters that form over water, like the ones off the coast of this town in Italy. Contrary to what you might think, the water in a waterspout comes not from below but from condensation in the storm cloud above. Even though it doesn't suck up much water, low pressure inside the funnel does have enough power to hose up fish. Imagine the forecast: cloudy with a chance of mackerel!

A Twister in Texas

Darkened by swirling dust and debris, a tornado rips across a deserted Texas plain. Although it looks extremely menacing, this powerful twister caused little damage. Like most tornadoes, it had a short life span—only 20 minutes from its birth as a dust whirl to its breakdown and disappearance.

Tornado Chasers

Standing out of harm's way, three brave scientists aim a portable Doppler radar directly at the whirling tornado. The measurements they take will help them learn more about tornadoes.

Tornadoes Close up

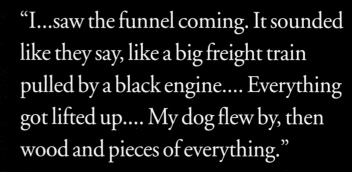

"I...saw the funnel coming. It sounded like they say, like a big freight train pulled by a black engine.... Everything got lifted up.... My dog flew by, then wood and pieces of everything."

Tornado victim, Arkansas

Smashing a house here, sparing a house there, a twister stamped across a Kansas town.

Stripped of its tail feathers, but with its dignity intact, a chicken is living proof of the unpredictable nature of tornadoes.

A 500-pound baby grand piano lies in a cornfield, tossed 396 m (1,300 ft.).

Like a bully on a rampage, a tornado slam-dunked the hoop at this midwestern school, trashed a few windows, ripped off part of the roof, and dashed away.

Picture Credits

Glossary of Terms

Air mass (air mass) A large body of air throughout which the temperature, surface pressure, and humidity are fairly constant.

Air pressure (air presh-ur) The weight of the atmosphere over a particular point; also called barometric pressure.

Atmosphere (at-muhss-fihr) The envelope of gases surrounding a planet or other celestial body. Earth's atmosphere is divided into five layers: exosphere, thermosphere, mesosphere, stratosphere, and troposphere.

Cirque (suhrk) A bowl-shaped, steep-walled mountain basin formed by erosion at the head of a glacier.

Cirrus clouds (seer-uhs kloudz) Thin, wispy clouds that form high in the atmosphere as their water vapor freezes into ice crystals.

Coal (kohl) A dark-brown to black natural, solid, burnable substance formed when plant remains fossilize under conditions of great pressure, high humidity, and lack of air.

Condensation (kon-den-say-shuhn) The changing of a vapor to a liquid.

Continental drift (kon-tuh-nen-tuhl drift) The theory that the continents ride on giant plates that have been moving very slowly across the surface of Earth for 300 million years.

Crystal (kriss-tuhl) A solid that has a definite internal atomic structure, producing a characteristic external shape and physical and optical prop-

erties; also, a clear, transparent mineral that looks like ice.

Cumulus clouds (kyoo-myuh-luhs kloudz) Dense, mid-level clouds that develop in mounded or towering shapes and signal fair weather.

Cyclone (sye-klone) A very violent windstorm with circular winds that move around a center of low pressure. Cyclones form over the ocean.

Element (el-uh-muhnt) One of the more than 100 basic substances from which all other things are made. An element is formed of only one kind of atom.

Erosion (i-roh-zhuhn) The wearing away of Earth's surface by natural agents, including wind, ocean waves, and glaciers.

Evaporation (i-vap-uh-ray-shuhn) The changing of liquid to a vapor.

Fetch (fech) The distance along open water or land over which the wind blows.

Firn (feern) A dense, tightly packed accumulation of powdery snow. With repeated melting and freezing and pressure from the overlying snow, the firn turns into glacial ice.

Fossil fuel (foss-uhl fyoo-uhl) Coal, oil, or natural gas. These fuels are the fossil remains of age-old plants and animals.

Front (fruhnt) A zone of atmospheric turbulence, formed when two air masses of different temperatures and humidities collide, resulting in stormy, changeable weather.

Glacier (glay-shur) A large mass of ice that survives for many years, slowly carving out the face of Earth.

Granite (gran-it) A coarse-grained, light-colored, igneous rock that is formed when magma cools underground. It is used for buildings and monuments.

Groundwater (ground-waw-tur) Water that accumulates in porous rock deep beneath Earth's surface.

Gulf Stream (guhlf streem) A warm, swift current in the Atlantic Ocean that flows from the Gulf of Mexico along the eastern coast of the United States and then northeast toward Europe.

Gyre (jire) A ringlike movement of ocean currents. The Gulf Stream is part of a large gyre carrying water around the Atlantic Ocean basin.

Haboob (hah-boob) A thick dust storm or sandstorm that blows in the deserts of North Africa and Arabia or on the plains of India.

High-pressure system (hye-presh-ur siss-tuhm) A whirling mass of cool, dry air that generally brings fair weather and light winds.

Humidity (hyoo-mid-i-tee) The amount of water vapor present in the air.

Hurricane (hur-uh-kane) A severe, swirling tropical storm with heavy rains and winds. Hurricanes begin over tropical seas.

Iceberg (eyess-berg) A massive body of land ice that has broken off from the end of a

glacier, and is afloat in the ocean.

Igneous rock (ig-nee-uhss rok) Rock that has crystallized from a molten state. Igneous rock is one of the three major kinds of rock; the others are sedimentary and metamorphic.

Kimberlite (kim-buhr-lite) A kind of rock that forms in narrow, pipelike volcanic chimneys and often contains diamonds.

Latent heat (lay-tuhnt heet) The heat required to change a liquid to a vapor without a change in temperature. It is also the heat released when a vapor changes to a liquid.

Lava (lah-vuh) Hot, molten rock that reaches the surface of Earth and erupts out of a volcano.

Liquid (lik-wid) A substance that is neither a solid nor a vapor. A liquid has molecules that move freely and takes the shape of the container in which it is put.

Loess (loh-uhss) A deposit of fine silt or dust that has been transported to its present location by the wind. It forms a highly fertile topsoil.

Low-pressure system (loh-presh-ur siss-tuhm) A whirling mass of warm, moist air that generally brings unsettled weather with strong winds.

Maelstrom (mayl-struhm) A large and violent whirlpool, caused when two or more currents collide. A famous maelstrom occurs off the coast of Norway.

Magma (**mag**-muh) Hot, molten rock generated within Earth.

Manganese nodules (**man**-guh-nees **noj**-ools) Black potato-sized masses found on the ocean floor that contain up to 34 percent manganese.

Mantle (**man**-tuhl) The layer of Earth between the crust and the outer core; the mantle reaches a depth of about 1,800 miles.

Marble (**mar**-buhl) A coarse-grained, crystalline metamorphic rock made from the action of heat and pressure on limestone.

Metamorphic rock (met-uh-**mor**-fik **rok**) A rock whose composition, structure, or texture has been transformed by heat and pressure. Metamorphic rock is one of the three major kinds of rock; the other two are igneous and sedimentary.

Meteorology (mee-tee-uh-**rol**-uh-jee) The science that studies the atmosphere and its phenomena, including weather and how to forecast it.

Mineral (**min**-ur-uhl) A natural inorganic substance with certain measurable properties, such as hardness, crystal structure, and specific gravity. There are about 2,000 known minerals on Earth.

Monsoon (mon-**soon**) A seasonal wind, found especially in Asia, that reverses direction between summer and winter and often brings heavy rains.

Oceanography (oh-shuh-**nog**-ruh-fee) The exploration and scientific study of the oceans, including marine life.

Oil (**oil**) A fossil fuel formed by the decomposition of microscopic marine plants and animals over millions of years.

Orogeny (o-**roj**-uh-nee) The creation of mountains by folding and faulting in Earth's crust. This is due to the interplay between Earth's moving plates.

Precipitation (pri-sip-i-**tay**-shuhn) General name for water in any form falling from clouds; includes rain, drizzle, hail, snow, and sleet.

Prevailing wind (pree-**vay**-ling **wind**) The directional wind that occurs more frequently than any other in a given location.

Pyroclastic flow (pye-roh-**klass**-tik **floh**) Hot, fast-moving cloud of gas, ash, and rock ejected explosively from a volcano.

Quartz (**kworts**) A hard, transparent mineral composed of silicon and oxygen; quartz is the most common of all minerals and is present in many rocks and soils.

Radiant energy (**ray**-dee-uhnt **en**-ur-jee) Energy in the form of waves, especially electromagnetic waves. X-rays, radio waves, heat, and light are forms of radiant energy.

Rock cycle (**rok sye**-kuhl) The constant movement of minerals through Earth's crust, due to the formation, disintegration, and reformation of rocks.

Sandstone (**sand**-stohn) A type of sedimentary rock formed of compressed sand particles.

Scattering (**skat**-ur-ing) The spread of a beam of particles or rays over a range of directions as a result of collisions or other physical interactions.

Sea (**see**) Any large body of salt water, smaller than an ocean, partly or almost wholly enclosed by land.

Sedimentary rock (sed-uh-**men**-tuh-ree rok) Rock formed from sediments that have been compacted and cemented together. One of the three major types of rock; the other two are igneous and metamorphic.

Spectrum (**spek**-truhm) In light, the band of colors formed when a beam of white light is broken up according to wavelengths, as when passing through a prism or striking water drops.

Stratus clouds (**strat**-uhss **kloudz**) Low-lying, sheetlike clouds that often produce a light drizzle.

Subduction The forcing of the oceanic part of one tectonic plate under the dry-land portion of another plate.

Tectonic plates (tek-**ton**-ik **playts**) Rigid pieces of Earth's crust and upper mantle that carry continents and ocean floor; tectonic plates move very slowly over the surface of the globe.

Tidal range (**tye**-duhl **raynj**) The difference in water level between high tide and low tide at a given place.

Tide (**tide**) The alternate rise and fall of the surface of oceans, seas, and bays caused by the gravitational pull of the Moon and, to a lesser de-gree, the Sun.

Tornado (tor-**nay**-doh) A violently rotating column of air that spins around a tube of low pressure. Tornadoes form over land.

Transpiration (transs-puh-**ray**-shuhn) The loss of water by evaporation from plant leaves through tiny pores in the leaves.

Tsunami (tsoo-**nah**-mee) A Japanese term for an unusually large ocean wave caused by an undersea earthquake, volcanic eruption, or rockslide.

Typhoon (tye-**foon**) A hurricane that occurs in eastern Asia.

Vapor (**vay**-pur) Faintly visible suspension of fine particles of matter in the air, as mist, fumes, fog, or smoke.

Water cycle (**waw**-tur **sye**-kuhl) The constant movement of water, by evaporation, condensation, and precipitation, between the oceans and land.

Wavelength (**wayv**-lengkth) The distance between one peak, or crest, of a wave and the next peak, or crest.

Weather (**weth**-ur) The state of the atmosphere in terms of the six meteorological elements: temperature, atmospheric pressure, wind, humidity, precipitation, and cloudiness.

Weathering (**weth**-ur-ing) The breaking down of rocks through contact with the atmosphere.

Wind (**wind**) The movement of air relative to the surface of Earth.

Index

Index

TIME-LIFE BOOKS

Time-Life Education, Inc. is a division of Time Life Inc.

TIME LIFE INC.

PRESIDENT and CEO: George Artandi
CHIEF OPERATING OFFICER: Mary Davis Holt

TIME-LIFE EDUCATION, INC.
PRESIDENT: Mary Davis Holt
MANAGING EDITOR: Mary J. Wright

Time-Life Student Library
PLANET EARTH

EDITOR: Jean Burke Crawford

Deputy Editor: Terrell Smith
Text Editor: Allan Fallow
Associate Editor/Research and Writing: Mary Saxton
Picture Coordinator: Lisa Groseclose
Page Makeup Specialist: Monika D. Lynde
Technical Artist: John Drummond

Designed by: Phillip Unetic and Lori Cohen, 3r1 Group

Special Contributors: Sara Mark (development), Patricia Daniels, Marge duMond, Susan McGrath, Susan Perry (text), Susan S. Blair, Patti Cass, Susie Kelly (research), Barbara Klein (index).
Copyeditor: Darcie Johnston
Correspondents: Maria Vincenza Aloisi (Paris), Christine Hinze (London), Christina Lieberman (New York).

Vice President of Marketing and Publisher: Rosalyn McPherson Andrews
Vice President of Sales: Robert F. Sheridan
Director of Book Production: Patricia Pascale
Director of Publishing Technology: Betsi McGrath
Director of Photography and Research: John Conrad Weiser
Marketing Manager: Michelle Stegmaier
Production Manager: Gertraude Schaefer
Quality Assurance Manager: James King
Chief Librarian: Louise D. Forstall
Direct Marketing Consultant: Barbara Erlandson

Consultants:

Joseph M. Bishop, Ph.D., is an adjunct professor at The Johns Hopkins University, teaching Environmental Science and Policy at the graduate school of Arts and Sciences. His background is in meteorology and oceanography.

Ronald Gird is a meteorologist for the National Weather Service, National Oceanic and Atmospheric Administration (NOAA). He has been with the Satellite Space Program of NOAA since 1972 and is currently Satellite and Space Flight Program Leader.

Dr. James F. Luhr is Research Geologist and Director of the Global Volcanism Program at the Smithsonian Institution's National Museum of Natural History. He is an authority on the volcanoes in Mexico and co-edited *Parícutin: The Volcano Born In A Mexican Cornfield.*

Dr. Hubert Miller is Professor of Geology at the Ludwig-Maximilian University of Munich. He specializes in the field of mountain building and is spending much of his time in the Alps, the South American Andes, and Antarctica to study formation and deformation of rocks and their correlation in time and space.

Fran Schwind is a sixth-grade science teacher at Edgar Allan Poe Middle School in Fairfax County, Va. Over a period of 18 years she has taught fifth, sixth, and seventh grade science in the Fairfax County Public School System.

Todd P. Stansbery is a lower school Lab Science Teacher and Student Activities Coordinator at St. Stephens & St. Agnes School in Alexandria, Va. Winner of the 1996 Alexandria Chamber of Commerce Excellence in Education award, he received a Masters in Environmental Science from The Johns Hopkins University, focusing mainly on life and earth sciences.

Dr. George C. Stephens, chairman of the geology department at the George Washington University in Washington, D.C., specializes in mountain-building processes and the evolution of glacial landscapes. Currently Dr. Stephens is studying the geologic evolution of the Andes Mountains.

Second printing 1998. Printed in U.S.A.
School and library distribution by Time-Life Education, P.O. Box 85026, Richmond, Virginia 23285-5026.
Telephone: 1-800-449-2010
Internet: WWW.TIMELIFEEDU.COM

TIME-LIFE is a trademark of Time Warner Inc. U.S.A.

Library of Congress Cataloging-in-Publication Data
Planet earth.
    p. cm. — (Time-Life student library)
    Includes bibliographical references and index.
    Summary: Describes the earth sciences and examines volcanoes, earthquakes, mountains, rivers, lakes, oceans, rocks, minerals, weather, and the atmosphere.
    ISBN 0-7835-1350-X
    1. Earth sciences—Juvenile literature. [1. Earth sciences.] I. Time-Life Books. II. Series.
QE29.P63   1997
550—dc21
                                    97-28566
                                      CIP
                                      AC

OTHER PUBLICATIONS

TIME-LIFE KIDS
Library of First Questions and Answers
A Child's First Library of Learning
I Love Math
Nature Company Discoveries
Understanding Science & Nature

HISTORY
What Life Was Like
The American Story
Voices of the Civil War
The American Indians
Lost Civilizations
Mysteries of the Unknown
Time Frame
The Civil War
Cultural Atlas

SCIENCE/NATURE
Voyage Through the Universe

DO IT YOURSELF
The Time-Life Complete Gardener
Home Repair and Improvement
The Art of Woodworking
Fix It Yourself

COOKING
Weight Watchers®, Smart Choice
Recipe Collection
Great Taste-Low Fat
Williams-Sonoma Kitchen Library

For information on and a full description of any of the Time-Life Books series listed above, please call 1-800-621-7026 or write:

Reader Information
Time-Life Customer Service
P.O. Box C-32068
Richmond, Virginia 23261-2068